20

To: Mrs. Howard

with love,

from

Zachary
Korte

Presented to:

_____

From:

_____

Date:

_____

God's Little Lessons for Teachers

Honor Books
Tulsa, Oklahoma

God's Little Lessons for Teachers
ISBN 1-56292-998-4
Copyright © 2001 by Honor Books
P.O. Box 55388
Tulsa, Oklahoma 74155

Introduction

Teaching is an extraordinary career. What other calling offers the opportunity to mold so many young lives? What an incredible privilege and responsibility! But sometimes this task may seem quite overwhelming.

That's when it's good to know that God's Word provides you with all the answers you will need to face a classroom full of questioning young faces. It is filled with encouragement and insight on every topic from anger to forgiveness, discouragement to joy, and many other real life issues.

God's Little Lessons for Teachers is specially designed with you in mind. It combines insightful scriptures with powerful devotional stories to help you successfully conquer each day. It will give you the inspiration you need to remain true to your calling and the Scriptural principles you desire to teach to the students who pass through your classroom.

It is our prayer that as you read through the pages of this book, you will discover all that God wants to do in and through your life.

Table of Contents

Anger 8

Anxiety 12

Attitude 16

Comfort 20

Commitment 24

Confidence 28

Courage...32

Death 36

Depression...40

Discouragement...................................44

Doubt 48

Example...52

Failure 54

Faith 58

Fear 62

Forgiveness 66

Friendship 70

Frustration...74

Giving 78

God's Love 82

Gossip 86

Guidance 90

Happiness 94

Honesty..98

Hope 102

Joy..106

Knowledge 110

Laughter 114
Loneliness 118
Love 120
Money/Materialism...............................124
Patience...128
Peace 132
Perseverance 136
Prayer 140
Priorities 144
Renewal...148
Restoration 152
Self-discipline......................................156
Self-pity 160
Shame 164
Speech 168
Spiritual Growth 172
Stability 176
Strength...180
Stress 184
Success 188
Temptation 192
Thankfulness 196
Truth...200
Wisdom 204
Work 208
Worry 212
Worship 216

GOD'S Little Lessons for Teachers

Anger

Wherefore, my beloved brethren, let every man
be swift to hear, slow to speak, slow to wrath:
For the wrath of man worketh not the
righteousness of God.

James 1:19-20 KJV

A gentle answer turns away wrath, but a harsh
word stirs up anger.

Proverbs 15:1

8   You yourselves are to put off all these: anger,
wrath, malice, blasphemy, filthy language
out of your mouth.

Colossians 3:8 NKJV

He who guards his lips guards his life, but he
who speaks rashly will come to ruin.

Proverbs 13:3

Roars and Screeches

A n old fable tells the story of a young lion and a cougar. Both were thirsty, and they both happened to arrive at the local watering hole at the same time. They immediately began to argue about who should satisfy his thirst first.

The argument became heated, and each decided he was due the privilege of being first to quench his thirst. Rulership of the territory was at stake! Pride was an issue! As they stubbornly confronted each other, their emotions turned to rage. Their roars and screeches could be heard for miles as they moved closer and closer to entangling in battle.

9

Then they both noticed strange shadows skirting across the ground. Both looked up at the same time. Circling overhead was a flock of vultures, waiting for the loser to fall. Quietly, the two beasts turned and walked away. The thought of being devoured was all they needed to end their quarrel.

Engaging in a shouting match with students over control of the classroom is ineffective and oftentimes dangerous. When you've reached your breaking point with a disruptive student, ask God to help you handle the situation with confidence and self-control.[1]

GOD'S Little Lessons for Teachers

Anger

An angry man stirs up strife, And a hot-tempered man abounds in transgression.

Proverbs 29:22 NASB

Do not make friends with a hot-tempered man, . . . or you may learn his ways and get yourself ensnared.

Proverbs 22:24-25

10

He that is slow to anger is better than the mighty; and he that ruleth his spirit than he that taketh a city.

Proverbs 16:32 KJV

If you stay calm, you are wise, but if you have a hot temper, you only show how stupid you are.

Proverbs 14:29 TEV

Steering Clear of Trouble

huck Givens admits that he was once a pro at getting angry with both traffic delays and the drivers who caused them. He had a habit of venting his anger by pounding on the steering wheel of his car, usually while saying, "Those idiots . . . what do they think they're doing? What is this, a parade?"

On many days, he admits that he worked himself from fervor to frenzy. The more frustrated he became, the harder he pounded on his steering wheel until his face turned bright red in anger. It didn't matter to him who else was in the car. He was convinced he was right and expressed himself freely: "Get out of my way! Don't you know I've got important things to do? If I had my way, nobody would drive on the highway when I'm using it!"

11

However, one day his attitude changed. While driving with a friend and "up to his hubcaps in traffic," he pounded soundly on the steering wheel, and—*crack*—it broke! In an instant, he rendered his car undrivable, and his anger dissolved into embarrassment.

In life and in the classroom, anger rarely solves a problem. In fact it usually just makes things worse. So the next time you are faced with an opportunity to let anger get the best of you, remember to think through the consequences first.[2]

GOD'S Little Lessons for Teachers

Anxiety

Do not be anxious about anything, but in everything, by prayer and petition, with thanksgiving, present your requests to God. And the peace of God, which transcends all understanding, will guard your hearts and your minds in Christ Jesus.

Philippians 4:6-7

For I, the LORD your God, hold your right hand; it is I who say to you, "Fear not, I will help you."

Isaiah 41:13 RSV

12

"These things I have spoken unto you, that in me ye might have peace. In the world ye shall have tribulation: but be of good cheer; I have overcome the world."

John 16:33 KJV

Therefore humble yourselves under the mighty hand of God, that He may exalt you in due time, casting all your care upon Him, for He cares for you.

1 Peter 5:6-7 NKJV

Letting Go

To let go doesn't mean to stop caring; it means I can't do it for someone else.

To let go is not to cut myself off; it's the realization that I don't control another.

To let go is not to enable, but to allow learning from natural consequences.

To let go is to admit powerlessness, which means the outcome is not in my hands.

To let go is not to try to change or blame another; I can only change myself.

To let go is not to care for, but to care about.

To let go is not to fix, but to be supportive.

13

To let go is not to be protective; it is to permit another to face reality.

To let go is not to deny, but to accept.

To let go is not to nag, scold, or argue, but to search out my own shortcomings and correct them.

To let go is not to criticize and regulate anyone, but to try to become what I dream I can be.

To let go is not to regret the past, but to grow and live for the future.

To let go is to fear less and love more.

Anonymous

You'll experience a lot less anxiety in life and in your classroom when you learn to let go.

GOD'S Little Lessons for Teachers

Anxiety

Cast thy burden upon the LORD, and he shall sustain thee.

Psalm 55:22 KJV

"Come to me, all you who are weary and burdened, and I will give you rest."

Matthew 11:28

"I will not abandon you as orphans—I will come to you."

John 14:18 NLT

14

Do you think anyone is going to be able to drive a wedge between us and Christ's love for us? There is no way! Not trouble, not hard times, not hatred, not hunger, not homelessness, not bullying threats, not backstabbing, not even the worst sins listed in Scripture.

Romans 8:35 THE MESSAGE

Looking Up

n her book *Glorious Intruder,* Joni Eareckson Tada tells about horseback riding with her older sisters when they were all children. She had a hard time keeping up with them because the pony she was riding was half the size of their mounts.

She didn't mind, but took it as a challenge—until they came to the edge of a river. She writes:

> My sisters on their big horses thought it was fun and exciting to cross the river at the deepest part. They never seemed to notice that my little pony sank quite a bit deeper. . . . It was scary, but I wasn't about to let them know. One crossing in particular sticks in my memory. . . . It had rained earlier that week and the river was brown and swollen. As our horses waded out toward midstream, I became transfixed staring at the swirling waters rushing around the legs of my pony. It made me scared and dizzy. I began to lose my balance in the saddle. The voice of my sister Jay finally broke through my panic. "Look up, Joni! Keep looking up!"

15

Focusing on her sister, Joni made it safely to the opposite shore.

As a teacher, it is important to keep your eyes on Jesus. In doing so, your fear and anxiety will slip away, enabling you to positively impact your students' lives.

GOD'S Little Lessons for Teachers

Attitude

As he thinks in his heart, so is he.

Proverbs 23:7 NKJV

A merry heart doeth good like a medicine: but a broken spirit drieth the bones.

Proverbs 17:22 KJV

Happy are those who fear the LORD. Yes, happy are those who delight in doing what he commands.

Psalm 112:1 NLT

16

When people are happy, they smile, but when they are sad, they look depressed.

Proverbs 15:13 TEV

Lighten Up

The great preacher Charles H. Spurgeon once emphasized to a preaching class that a speaker's facial expressions should harmonize with the sermon. He suggested that "when you speak of Heaven, let your face light up, let it be irradiated with a heavenly gleam, let your eyes shine with reflected glory. But when you speak of hell, well, then your ordinary face will do."

While we may think it fake to "force" an attitude of cheerfulness or a facial expression, such as a smile, scientific documentation has proved that sustaining a cheerful expression actually uses less muscle power than maintaining a frown. Researchers also note that an optimistic, upbeat attitude can more easily defuse pressure and stress than an attitude of pessimism. And medical science has long recognized the profound, instantaneous benefits of laughter on virtually every important organ in the human body. Even forced laughter reduces health-sapping tension while it simultaneously relaxes the muscles and exercises the organs. In fact, three minutes of sustained laughter will exercise your body as much as thirty minutes on a rowing machine.

17

Teach your students to lighten up their outlooks to relieve nervousness, tension, and fatigue. Indulge in a daily dose of laughter with them so that they will discover its beneficial effects, both mentally and physically.

GOD'S Little Lessons for Teachers

Attitude

[Jesus] said to them, "Truly I say to you, if you have faith as a mustard seed, you shall say to this mountain, 'Move from here to there,' and it shall move; and nothing shall be impossible to you."

Matthew 17:20 NASB

Faith comes by hearing, and hearing by the word of God.

Romans 10:17 NKJV

18   The boy's father exclaimed, "I do believe; help me overcome my unbelief!"

Mark 9:24

To have faith is to be sure of the things we hope for, to be certain of the things we cannot see.

Hebrews 11:1 TEV

Awful Attitude

heryl continually complained that she didn't make enough money, couldn't afford the things she wanted, and therefore, wasn't ever going to amount to anything. A counselor said to her, "You're throwing your energy away complaining instead of using it to get ahead."

"But you don't understand. The job is the problem, not me," Cheryl countered.

The counselor said, "Your low-paying job may be a problem, and your boss may demand too much, but if you are continually that upset, you are causing yourself more harm than either the job or the boss."

19

"What can I do?" she asked.

The counselor said, "You can't control your boss or the job, but you can control how you *feel* about them. Change your attitude."

Cheryl took her advice. When she stopped whining about her life, people around her noticed. She got a promotion, and with her new job status, she was more marketable. Within several months, she was transferred out of the department into a position with even higher pay and a more supportive boss.

Awful is a state of *attitude*. Teach your students that a change in attitude will change the state of things!

GOD'S Little Lessons for Teachers

Comfort

Trust in him at all times, O people; pour out your hearts to him, for God is our refuge.

Psalm 62:8

You have turned for me my mourning into dancing; You have put off my sackcloth and clothed me with gladness.

Psalm 30:11 NKJV

20

[Jesus said]: "Therefore you too now have sorrow; but I will see you again, and your heart will rejoice, and no one takes your joy away from you."

John 16:22 NASB

When times are good, be happy; but when times are bad, consider: God has made the one as well as the other.

Ecclesiastes 7:14

It Came to Pass

A vibrant old woman astounded everyone with her consistent cheerfulness even though she seemed to have abundant troubles and few pleasures. When she was asked the secret of her upbeat personality, she replied, "Well, the Bible says often, 'And it came to pass'—not 'and it came to stay!'"

One of life's greatest lessons is that we are all "works in progress." Your students won't be the same at the end of the year as they are on the first day of school. Neither will you be the same teacher!

A little girl was once asked by her Sunday school teacher, "Who made you?"

21

She quickly answered, "Well, God made a part of me."

The teacher asked, "What do you mean, God made a part of you?"

She replied, "Well, God made me real little, and I just growed the rest myself."

Certainly God makes himself available to help us in our growth process, but He also expects us to grow through the decisions we make, the challenges we undertake, and the effort we put out. Embrace the changes that come your way. They are part of God's ongoing process for you—both as a teacher and as a person.[3]

GOD'S Little Lessons for Teachers

Comfort

Many are the sorrows of the wicked; But he who trusts in the LORD, lovingkindness shall surround him.

Psalm 32:10 NASB

"Blessed are you who hunger now, for you will be satisfied. Blessed are you who weep now, for you will laugh."

Luke 6:21

22
The eyes of the LORD are on those who fear him, on those whose hope is in his unfailing love.

Psalm 33:18

You are my hiding place; You shall preserve me from trouble; You shall surround me with songs of deliverance.

Psalm 32:7 NKJV

The Compost Pile

ohn H. Timmerman once wrote,

In the back corner of my yard, partitioned by a rose bed and a 40-year-old lilac bush, rests a pile, 8 feet long, 4 feet wide, and 4 feet high—my compost pile. Old-fashioned chicken wire stapled to well-anchored stakes holds it in place. Into it I toss every bit of yard scrap and a heavy dose of kitchen scrap . . . a bit of lime now and then . . . and an occasional handful of fertilizer. The compost pile burns hot, never smells, and each October yields about 70 bushels of fine black dirt, dark as midnight, moist and flaky, that I spread in the garden.

23

Each night when we go to bed, we are wise to turn the day's "garbage" over to the Lord in prayer and trust God to transform our mistakes and errors into something useful. And indeed He does. The garbage of our lives often becomes the compost for spiritual fruit.

The key is not "sleeping on a problem," but rather choosing to sleep *in spite* of a problem. We must trust God to turn a day of classroom disaster into a dawning of hope.[4]

GOD'S Little Lessons for Teachers

Commitment

As you therefore have received Christ Jesus the Lord, so walk in Him, rooted and built up in Him and established in the faith, as you have been taught, abounding in it with thanksgiving.

Colossians 2:6-7 NKJV

Dear brothers and sisters, stand firm and keep a strong grip on everything we taught you both in person and by letter.

2 Thessalonians 2:15 NLT

24

Commit your way to the LORD; trust in him and he will do this: He will make your righteousness shine like the dawn, the justice of your cause like the noonday sun.

Psalms 37:5-6

So if you find life difficult because you're doing what God said, take it in stride. Trust him. He knows what he's doing, and he'll keep on doing it.

1 Peter 4:19 THE MESSAGE

Commit to Hope

nita Septimus has worked as a social worker for HIV-infected children since 1985. In the first few months she worked with her tiny clients, three of them died. Despair began to overwhelm her. She made a commitment to stick with the job for three more months, during which time she could not get a friend's words out of her thoughts, "You have not chosen a pretty profession."

She had to admit her friend was right. She decided, at that point, to accept the reality of her work and simply do what she could to help families make the most of what remained of their children's lives. And as a result of this decision, she is still working there today.

25

Over the last ten years, her clinic has grown considerably. Today, Anita and her staff care for more than 300 families with AIDS children. They go into their homes, teach infection prevention, and help parents plan for the future.

One AIDS baby wasn't expected to see her first birthday, but she recently celebrated her tenth. Such "long-term" clients give back to Anita what she terms "an indestructible sense of hope"—a precious gift!

When you make a similar commitment to sow hope into the lives of your students, you will reap back tremendous hope for your own life as well.

GOD'S Little Lessons for Teachers

Commitment

Let your heart therefore be loyal to the LORD our God, to walk in His statutes and keep His commandments, as at this day.

1 Kings 8:61 NKJV

Commit your work to the LORD, and then your plans will succeed.

Proverbs 16:3 NLT

Now all has been heard; here is the conclusion of the matter: Fear God and keep his commandments, for this is the whole duty of man.

Ecclesiastes 12:13

Turn your back on evil, work for the good and don't quit. GOD loves this kind of thing, never turns away from his friends.

Psalm 37:27 THE MESSAGE

Hull House

ane was only seven years old when she visited a shabby street in a nearby town and, seeing ragged children there, announced that she wanted to build a big house so poor children would have a place to play. As a young adult, Jane and a friend visited Toynbee Hall in London, where they saw educated people helping the poor by living among them.

She and her friend returned to Chicago, restored an old mansion, and moved in! There they cared for children of working mothers and held sewing and cooking classes. Older boys and girls had clubs at the mansion. An art gallery as well as public music, reading, and craft rooms were created in the mansion. Her dream came true!

27

Jane didn't stop there. She spoke up for people who couldn't speak for themselves. She was eventually awarded an honorary degree from Yale. President Theodore Roosevelt dubbed her "America's most useful citizen," and she was awarded the Nobel Prize for Peace.

No matter how famous she became, however, Jane Addams remained a resident of Hull House. She died there, in the heart of the slum she had come to call home.

When we commit our dreams and plans to the Lord, He will see to it that they come to pass.

GOD'S Little Lessons for Teachers

Confidence

We are always confident, knowing that while we are at home in the body we are absent from the Lord. For we walk by faith, not by sight.

2 Corinthians 5:6-7 NKJV

Let us then approach the throne of grace with confidence, so that we may receive mercy and find grace to help us in our time of need.

Hebrews 4:16

28   We have confidence to enter the holy place by the blood of Jesus.

Hebrews 10:19 NASB

The Lord shall be your confidence, firm and strong, and shall keep your foot from being caught [in a trap or some hidden danger].

Proverbs 3:26 AMP

Always Useful to God

n *Glorious Intruder,* Joni Eareckson Tada writes the following about Diane who suffers from multiple sclerosis:

In her quiet sanctuary, Diane turns her head slightly on the pillow toward the corkboard on the wall. Her eyes scan each thumbtacked card and list. Each photo. Every torn piece of paper carefully pinned in a row. The stillness is broken as Diane begins to murmur. She is praying.

Some would look at Diane—stiff and motionless—and shake their heads . . . "What a shame. Her life has no meaning. She can't really do anything." But Diane is confident, convinced her life is significant. Her labor of prayer counts. She pushes back the kingdom of darkness that blackens the alleys and streets of east Los Angeles. She aids homeless mothers, single parents, abused children, despondent teenagers, handicapped boys, and dying and forgotten old people. Diane is on the front lines, advancing the gospel of Christ, holding up weak saints, inspiring doubting believers, energizing other prayer warriors, and delighting her Lord and Savior.

29

What a difference you can make in your students' lives if you have confidence in God's desire to use you! God is willing and able to use you regardless of your ability or inability—He always has a plan!

GOD'S Little Lessons for Teachers

Confidence

Blessed is the man who trusts in the LORD,
whose confidence is in him.

Jeremiah 17:7

This is the confidence we have in approaching God:
that if we ask anything according to his will, he
hears us. And if we know that he hears us—
whatever we ask—we know that we have what
we asked of him.

1 John 5:14-15

30

In him and through faith in him we may approach
God with freedom and confidence.

Ephesians 3:12

We have confidence before God and receive
from him anything we ask, because we obey
his commands and do what pleases him.

1 John 3:21-22

He's Holding You

Many years ago, a young woman who felt called into the ministry was accepted into a well-known seminary. There were only two other women enrolled there, and her very presence seemed to make her male classmates uncomfortable. She felt isolated. To make matters worse, many of her professors were doing their best to destroy her faith rather than build it up. Even her private devotions seemed dry and lonely.

At Christmas break she sought her father's counsel. "How can I be strong in my resolve and straight in my theology with all that I face there?"

Her father took a pencil from his pocket and laid it on the palm of his hand. "Can that pencil stand upright by itself?" he asked her.

"No," she replied. Then her father grasped the pencil in his hand and held it in an upright position.

"Ah," she said, "but you are holding it now."

"Daughter," he replied, "your life is like this pencil. But Jesus Christ is the One who can hold you." The young woman took her father's pencil and returned to seminary.

Whatever difficulties you may confront in your classroom, you can be confident that it is God who holds you in His hands. His strength holds you up and enables you to face anything that comes your way.

31

GOD'S Little Lessons for Teachers

Courage

Don't be afraid, for I am with you. Do not be dismayed, for I am your God. I will strengthen you. I will help you. I will uphold you with my victorious right hand.

Isaiah 41:10 NLT

Be strong, and let your heart take courage,
All you who hope in the LORD.

Psalm 31:24 NASB

32   Be on your guard; stand firm in the faith;
be men of courage; be strong.

1 Corinthians 16:13

The fear of man brings a snare, But whoever trusts in the LORD shall be safe.

Proverbs 29:25 NKJV

The Road Not Traveled

Some three hundred and fifty years ago, a shipload of pioneers landed on the northeast coast of America. The first year, they established a town. The next year, they elected a town government. During the third year, the town government revealed plans to build a road five miles west into the wilderness.

In the fourth year, the people tried to impeach their government because they thought it a waste of public money to construct a road five miles westward into an unknown territory. United, they voiced the opinion, "Why go there?"

33

These people had once had no trouble envisioning their own travel across three-thousand miles of ocean or setting their minds on overcoming the great hardships they knew such a voyage and new life would entail. But in four short years, they could not see five miles out of town! They had lost their pioneering spirit and their vision for what might be achieved.

We lose heart any time we allow a difficult situation to rob us of our God-given vision to see a better tomorrow, to see a failing student succeeding, to see a task becoming easier, or to see talent emerging from a quiet and withdrawn child.

Ask God to renew your vision and your courage.[5]

GOD'S Little Lessons for Teachers

Courage

The LORD is my light and my salvation; whom shall I fear? When evil men come to destroy me, they will stumble and fall! Yes, though a mighty army marches against me, my heart shall know no fear! I am confident that God will save me.

Psalms 27:1-3 TLB

He gives power to the tired and worn out, and strength to the weak.

Isaiah 40:29 TLB

34

That is why we can say without any doubt or fear, "The Lord is my Helper and I am not afraid of anything that mere man can do to me."

Hebrews 13:6 TLB

Overwhelming victory is ours through Christ who loved us enough to die for us.

Romans 8:37 TLB

Be Strong and Courageous

apoleon called Marshall Ney the bravest man he had ever known. Yet Ney's knees trembled so badly one morning before a battle, he had difficulty mounting his horse. When he was finally in the saddle, he shouted contemptuously down at his limbs, "Shake away, knees! You would shake worse than that if you knew where I am going to take you."

Courage is not a matter of being unafraid. It is a matter of taking action even when you are afraid!

Courage is more than shouting with sheer bravado, "I can do this!" and launching out with a "do-or-die" attitude over some reckless dare.

35

True courage is manifest when you choose to take a difficult or even dangerous course of action simply because it is the right thing to do. Courage is looking beyond yourself to what is best for another.

The Source of all courage is the Holy Spirit, our Comforter. It is His very nature to remain at our side, helping us. When we welcome Him into our lives and He compels us to do something, we can confidently believe that He will be right there, helping us accomplish whatever task He has called us to do.

GOD'S Little Lessons for Teachers

Death

We know that in everything God works for good with those who love him, who are called according to his purpose.

Romans 8:28 RSV

I am convinced that nothing can ever separate us from his love. Death can't, and life can't. The angels can't, and the demons can't. Our fears for today, our worries about tomorrow, and even the powers of hell can't keep God's love away. Whether we are high above the sky or in the deepest ocean, nothing in all creation will ever be able to separate us from the love of God that is revealed in Christ Jesus our Lord.

Romans 8:38-39 NLT

36

If we live, we live to the Lord; and if we die, we die to the Lord. So, whether we live or die, we belong to the Lord.

Romans 14:8

The bodies we now have are weak and can die. But they will be changed into bodies that are eternal. Then the Scriptures will come true, "Death has lost the battle! Where is its victory? Where is its sting?"

1 Corinthians 15:54-55 CEV

Silver Bells

isters Pauline and Mary always were close. They married and set up households within blocks of each other. Then in 1986, their lives changed. she was told she had breast cancer. Although radiation and chemotherapy left her fatigued, Pauline had unflagging optimism. She decided, "If my life is going to be shorter, I want it to be better." She continued to live her life fully!

As Pauline approached her fifty-eighth birthday, Mary and a friend commissioned a piece of jewelry in her honor—a tulip-shaped sterling-silver bell with a tiny chime inside, symbolic of the church bell choir in which Pauline played. Through tears Mary told her sister that she was going to have more bells made to sell, with the proceeds donated to cancer research.

37

Even after Pauline's death in June 1996, Mary continued to sell the bells. At last count, more than two thousand bells had been sold, raising more than $25,000 for cancer research. Mary has said, "Although cancer would ultimately take her body, Pauline refused to let it take her life!"

The seed of something good lies at the heart of every tragedy. Part of your challenge as a teacher is to find this seed and help it grow![6]

GOD'S Little Lessons for Teachers

Death

To all who mourn in Israel, he will give beauty for ashes, joy instead of mourning, praise instead of despair.

Isaiah 61:3 NLT

"Blessed are those who mourn, for they will be comforted."

Matthew 5:4

38

As the sufferings of Christ abound in us, so our consolation also abounds through Christ.

2 Corinthians 1:5 NKJV

Laugh with your happy friends when they're happy; share tears when they're down.

Romans 12:15 THE MESSAGE

Choosing Life

"Life is a test," Marnita Lloyd told her fellow classmates and teachers during graduation exercises at Detroit's Denby Technical and Preparatory High School. "You either pass or fail—it's up to you."

Marnita went on to a full scholarship at Wayne State University, but the road to academic achievement for this valedictorian had been marked by plenty of setbacks and obstacles. When she was eleven, her brother was killed in a drug dispute. When she was sixteen, her mother died of heart disease. During her senior year, a sixteen-year-old friend was fatally stabbed at his locker, and an eighteen-year-old friend was gunned down at a church carnival.

39

Marnita chose to continue attending classes rather than get involved in the commotion of the school slaying. She chose to stay home and study rather than participate in a neighborhood antiviolence parade after the carnival murder. "Those [parades] are good," she said, "but it won't help me study for my government test." Marnita kept her eyes on her personal goal: a medical career as an obstetrician-gynecologist. She chose to place her emphasis on new life instead of death.

If chaos is swirling in your classroom, set your students' sights on a higher goal.[7]

Depression

In my great trouble I cried to the Lord and he answered me; from the depths of death I called, and Lord, you heard me!

Jonah 2:2 TLB

Answer me quickly, O LORD; my spirit fails. Do not hide your face from me or I will be like those who go down to the pit. Let the morning bring me word of your unfailing love, for I have put my trust in you. Show me the way I should go, for to you I lift up my soul.

Psalms 143:7-8

40

I will refresh the weary and satisfy the faint.

Jeremiah 31:25

The LORD also will be a refuge for the oppressed, A refuge in times of trouble.

Psalm 9:9 NKJV

Overcomers

n 1980, Mount Saint Helens erupted, and the Pacific Northwest shuddered under its devastating impact. Forests were destroyed by fire. Rivers were choked with debris. Fish and other wildlife died. Toxic fumes filled the air, and reporters ominously predicted that acid rain would develop from the ash-laden clouds. The future for the area seemed bleak.

Nevertheless, less than a year after the eruption, scientists discovered that despite the fact that the rivers had been clogged with hot mud, volcanic ash, and floating debris, some of the salmon and steelhead had managed to survive. By using alternate streams and waterways, some of which were less than six inches deep, the fish returned home to spawn.

41

Within a few short years, the fields, lakes, and rivers surrounding Mount Saint Helens teemed with life. The water and soil seemed to benefit from the nutrients supplied by the exploding volcano. Even the mountain itself began to show signs of new vegetation.

Challenges in your classroom can enrich you and make you stronger. Trouble may only be the means to show you a different way to go, a different way to teach. It may be an opportunity to start afresh. Regardless of the challenges you face, always remember that you are God's creation, and you were designed to overcome!

GOD'S Little Lessons for Teachers

Depression

We have troubles all around us, but we are not defeated. We do not know what to do, but we do not give up the hope of living. We are persecuted, but God does not leave us. We are hurt sometimes, but we are not destroyed.

2 Corinthians 4:8-9 NCV

Cast your burden upon the LORD, and He will sustain you; He will never allow the righteous to be shaken.

Psalm 55:22 NASB

42

GOD IS OUR refuge and strength, a tested help in times of trouble.

Psalm 46:1 TLB

[Jesus said]: "In this world you will have trouble. But take heart! I have overcome the world."

John 16:33

The Fog of Depression

On a cool morning in July of 1952, Florence Chadwick waded into the waters off of Catalina Island, intending to swim the channel to the California coast. Though an experienced long-distance swimmer, Florence knew this swim would be difficult. The water was numbingly cold, and the fog was so thick she could hardly see the boat that carried her trainer.

Florence swam for more than fifteen hours. Several times she could sense sharks swimming next to her in the inky waters. Rifles were fired from the trainer's boat to help keep the sharks at bay. Yet when Florence looked around her, all she could see was the fog. When she finally asked to be lifted from the water, she was only a half-mile from her goal. In a later interview Florence admitted that it wasn't the cold, fear, or exhaustion that caused her to fail in her attempt to swim the Catalina Channel. It was the fog.

As a teacher, the struggles you face can sometimes cloak you in a fog of depression. Remember, even if you can't see the end of your trouble, press on. God hasn't brought you this far to leave you. He is standing there just outside the fog, waiting for your call.

GOD'S Little Lessons for Teachers

Discouragement

My mouth would encourage you; comfort from my lips would bring you relief.

Job 16:5

You are my hiding place from every storm of life; you even keep me from getting into trouble! You surround me with songs of victory.

Psalm 32:7 TLB

44

Those who know you, LORD, will trust you; you do not abandon anyone who comes to you.

Psalm 9:10 TEV

When life is good, enjoy it. But when life is hard, remember: God gives good times and hard times.

Ecclesiastes 7:14 NCV

You Mustn't Quit

When things go wrong, as they sometimes will,
When the road you're trudging seems all uphill,
When the funds are low and the debts are high
And you want to smile, but you have to sigh,
When care is pressing you down a bit,
Rest! If you must—but never quit.
Life is queer, with its twists and turns,
As every one of us sometimes learns,
And many a failure turns about
When he might have won if he'd stuck it out;
Stick to your task, though the pace seems slow.   45
You may succeed with one more blow.
Success is failure turned inside out,
The silver tint of the clouds of doubt.
And you never can tell how close you are,
It may be near when it seems afar;
So stick to the fight when you're hardest hit.
It's when things seem worst that
YOU MUSTN'T QUIT.

—Unknown

GOD'S Little Lessons for Teachers

Discouragement

We gladly suffer, because we know that suffering helps us to endure. And endurance builds character, which gives us a hope that will never disappoint us. All of this happens because God has given us the Holy Spirit, who fills our hearts with his love.

Romans 5:3-5 CEV

[Love] always protects, always trusts, always hopes, always perseveres.

1 Corinthians 13:7

46

Blessed is the man who endures trial, for when he has stood the test he will receive the crown of life which God has promised to those who love him.

James 1:12 RSV

May the Lord direct your hearts into God's love and Christ's perseverance.

2 Thessalonians 3:5

A Heavenly Ladder

ll of her life, Sarah Flower Adams had dreamed of becoming a great actress. She had worked and studied toward that goal, and at last she had realized her ambition. She scored a dramatic triumph as Lady MacBeth and was hailed as a great actress. But then a devastating illness made her an invalid. For three years, she did little except lie in her bed and read her Bible and books about saints and martyrs. She also wrote poems, mostly on religious themes.

One day, her minister came to visit and found Sarah feeling sorry for herself. He quietly took her Bible from the shelf and opened it to the story of Jacob's vision of a ladder extending into Heaven. Immediately, Sarah saw the parallel to her own life. She saw the darkness, the dream, the awakening, the sunshine, the triumph, the joy. She saw that each step of her suffering and affliction was a step that could bring her nearer to Heaven, nearer to God. Almost without effort, she wrote all afternoon. The poem she produced became one of the world's most beloved hymns: "Nearer, My God, To Thee."

47

God can provide a calm center to the fiercest storm. Ask Him to create one in your heart and in your classroom today.[8]

GOD'S Little Lessons for Teachers

Doubt

[Jesus said]: "Stop your doubting, and believe!"

John 20:27 TEV

God has said, "I will never, never fail you nor forsake you."

Hebrews 13:5 TLB

[Jesus said]: "Truly I say to you, whoever says to this mountain, 'Be taken up and cast into the sea,' and does not doubt in his heart, but believes that what he says is going to happen, it shall be granted him."

48

Mark 11:23 NASB

Why are you downcast, O my soul? Why so disturbed within me? Put your hope in God, for I will yet praise him, my Savior and my God.

Psalm 42:11

Don't Doubt; Have Faith

hile walking down a road one day, a turtle fell into a pothole in the center of a country road. He spun his little legs but couldn't free himself. A rabbit-friend came hopping along and offered assistance, but no matter what they tried, the turtle remained stuck in the muddy hole.

"It's no use," the turtle finally said. "There's no help for me." Various other animal friends passed his way, but the turtle refused their help, believing his destiny was sealed in the muck of the hole in which he had fallen. He sighed, "It's hopeless" and pulled his head inside his shell.

49

Then he heard a rumble. And peeking from his shell, he spotted a tractor heading straight for the pothole in which he sat. Without another thought, he scrambled out of the hole and across the road to safety.

Later that day, some of his animal friends saw him and asked, "How did you get free? We thought you couldn't get out of that pothole."

The turtle replied, "Oh, I couldn't . . . but then I had to!"

Don't wait for a crisis to develop in your classroom before you decide to take action on a problem or make a difficult decision. Act now. You'll save yourself stress and panic later.[9]

GOD'S Little Lessons for Teachers

Doubt

The one who doubts is like the surf of the sea driven and tossed by the wind.

James 1:6 NASB

Let us hold firmly to the hope that we have confessed, because we can trust God to do what he promised.

Hebrews 10:23 NCV

50

[Jesus said]: "If you have faith as a mustard seed, you will say to this mountain, 'Move from here to there,' and it will move; and nothing will be impossible for you."

Matthew 17:20 NKJV

Be merciful to those who doubt; snatch others from the fire and save them.

Jude 1:22-23

Stopping the Rain

urgeon Viggo Olsen was eager to build a hospital for the Bangladeshi people, especially after watching hundreds die of typhoid and cholera in the wake of a devastating typhoon. When he laid the official forms on the desk of the chief surveyor, however, the man laughed. "It will be impossible for us to survey tomorrow," he said, reminding Olsen of the monsoon season. Olsen insisted, but the official only shrugged and said, "It has been raining for days, and it will rain for days to come."

Olsen had seen other obstacles moved. He replied, "God will take care of the rain."

51

That night, Olsen and a companion prayed urgently for God to stop the rain. It rained all night and was raining in the morning when they went to the surveyor's office. Although they protested loudly, the crew agreed to go with Olsen on the thirty-two mile trip to the hospital site. As they drove, the rains only intensified, but soon the rain stopped, and a patch of blue sky emerged. Half an hour after arriving at the site, the sloping land had drained enough for the surveyors to do their work!

Never doubt the power of prayer! You may not be able to move mountains in your school—but God can.[10]

GOD'S Little Lessons for Teachers

Example

"I have set you an example that you should do as I have done for you."

John 13:15

Command and teach these things. Don't let anyone look down on you because you are young, but set an example for the believers in speech, in life, in love, in faith and in purity.

1 Timothy 4:11-12

52   If you suffer for doing good and you endure it, this is commendable before God. To this you were called, because Christ suffered for you, leaving you an example, that you should follow in his steps.

1 Peter 2:20-21

These things occurred as examples to keep us from setting our hearts on evil things.

1 Corinthians 10:6

For God Alone

ella Reese, singer and star of the TV show *Touched by an Angel*, considers Mahalia Jackson to have been her greatest teacher and mentor. As a teenager, she had the privilege of touring with Mahalia. On one occasion, Della recalls singing with all her might to wild applause. Then Mahalia rose and began to moan deep and low until she finally broke out singing, "Precious Lord, Take My Hand." She sang the entire song seated, speaking directly and only to God.

The audience responded with reverence and awe. Della thought, *What is it that she has that I don't have?*

53

After her third tour with Mahalia, she concluded that Mahalia was actually worshiping God, while she, on the other hand, was simply performing. Della's mother expressed it this way: "When Mahalia sings, you can feel God in her."

Mahalia expressed it a little differently: "Deloreese," she said, "you are not in competition. You are in God's service." This was a lesson Della never forgot, and a lesson she used throughout her life.

A teacher teaches character by example, not lecture. A student learns character by following and imitating, not memorizing.[11]

GOD'S Little Lessons for Teachers

Failure

I am very happy to brag about my weaknesses.
Then Christ's power can live in me.

2 Corinthians 12:9 NCV

Our High Priest is not one who cannot feel
sympathy for our weaknesses. . . . Let us have
confidence, then, and approach God's throne,
where there is grace. There we will receive mercy
and find grace to help us just when we need it.

Hebrews 4:15–16 TEV

54

If we believe not, yet he abideth faithful: he
cannot deny himself.

2 Timothy 2:13 KJV

Plans go wrong for lack of advice; many
counselors bring success.

Proverbs 15:22 NLT

Live Your Dream

obert D. Ballard is a man accustomed to
looking for things other people have
"lost." To date he has led or participated
in nearly one hundred deep-sea
expeditions. Among the "lost" things he has
found are the *R.M.S. Titanic,* the German
battleship *Bismarck,* and eleven warships that were
part of a fleet lost at Guadalcanal.

Did Ballard find these ships on his first try? No.
As he once said in a commencement address, "My
first voyage to find the *Titanic* ended in failure. My
first expedition to find the *Bismarck* failed as well.
The test you must pass is not whether you fall
down or not, but whether you can get back up."

55

Ballard also noted, "Every major adventure I
have been on over the years has tested me severely
with violent storms and lost equipment. . . . The
hardest tests of all . . . look to see how
determined you are to live your dream, how
strong is your heart."

If you truly believe that God has called you to
teach, never let go of your dream. Always walk
toward the next horizon. Consider failure only as an
opportunity to regroup and strengthen yourself.[12]

GOD'S Little Lessons for Teachers

Failure

At least there is hope for a tree: If it is cut down, it will sprout again, and its new shoots will not fail. Its roots may grow old in the ground and its stump die in the soil, yet at the scent of water it will bud and put forth shoots like a plant.

Job 14:7-9

And the Lord said, "Simon, Simon, behold, Satan hath desired to have you, that he may sift you as wheat: But I have prayed for thee, that thy faith fail not: and when thou art converted, strengthen thy brethren."

Luke 22:31-32 KJV

We can rejoice, too, when we run into problems and trials, for we know that they are good for us— they help us learn to endure. And endurance develops strength of character in us, and character strengthens our confident expectation of salvation.

Romans 5:3-4 NLT

We never give up. Our bodies are gradually dying, but we ourselves are being made stronger each day.

2 Corinthians 4:16 CEV

Guess These Top Ten Failures of All Time (answers below):

1. The engineer who neglected to design a reverse gear in the first car he manufactured.
2. The group turned down by Decca Records because "guitars are on their way out."
3. The illustrator told by his newspaper editor to pursue another line of work.
4. The skinny kid who hated the way he looked and was always being beat up by bullies.
5. The seriously ill, deeply in debt composer who in desperation wrote an oratorio in a few hours.
6. The obese, bald, deformed eccentric who became a reclusive thinker.

57

7. The orchestra conductor-composer who made his greatest contributions after becoming deaf.
8. The politician who lost his first seven elections.
9. The boy everyone thought was mute because his stutter was so bad he never spoke until he was a teenager.
10. The woman born deaf and blind who became a great writer and philanthropist, and once said, "I thank God for my handicaps."

Answers: 1. Henry Ford. 2. The Beatles. 3. Walt Disney. 4. Charles Atlas. 5. George Frederick Handel *(The Messiah)*. 6. Socrates. 7. Ludwig von Beethoven. 8. Abraham Lincoln. 9. James Earl Jones. 10. Helen Keller.

Our greatest failures can produce our greatest successes.

GOD'S Little Lessons for Teachers

Faith

What is faith? It is the confident assurance that what we hope for is going to happen. It is the evidence of things we cannot yet see.

Hebrews 11:1 NLT

Above all, taking the shield of faith, wherewith ye shall be able to quench all the fiery darts of the wicked.

Ephesians 6:16 KJV

58

We walk by faith, not by sight.

2 Corinthians 5:7 NKJV

"Everything is possible for him who believes."

Mark 9:23

The Exact Hour

n *God: A Biography,* Steven Mosley tells a story about Robert Foss and his Aunt Lana, who experienced a vision while praying. Upon reflection and research, they concluded this "picture from God" was of a quiet cove near the Quinault Indian reservation.

Since the family had clothes to deliver to the reservation, Robert and his aunt decided to deliver them immediately. On the way, they found the exact spot Aunt Lana had seen in her vision. However, nothing unusual happened when they stopped at the beach she had seen.

59

Upon arrival at the reservation, an old Indian grandmother said happily, "You've come! I've been expecting you." As they unloaded the clothes, she told about the trouble in her family and the lack of warm clothing for her grandchildren. One day, she had gone to a quiet place on the beach to ask for God's help. As they compared notes, they discovered her prayer had been at the exact day and hour the "picture" first came to Aunt Lana's mind!

Every teacher has finite vision, and is unable to see all that is going on backstage in God's unfolding plan. We need to keep our attention on the current assignment and then trust God daily that He is arranging all things for eternal benefit—both in our lives and in the lives of our students.[13]

GOD'S Little Lessons for Teachers

Faith

When I look at the night sky and see the work of you fingers—the moon and the stars you have set in place—what are mortals that you should think of us, mere humans that you should care for us? For you made us only a little lower than God, and you crowned us with glory and honor.

Psalms 8:3-5 NLT

Let love and faithfulness never leave you; bind them around your neck, write them on the tablet of your heart.

Proverbs 3:3

60

Every child of God can defeat the world, and our faith is what gives this victory.

1 John 5:4 CEV

"His master said to him, 'Well done, good and faithful servant; you have been faithful over a little, I will set you over much; enter into the joy of your master.'"

Matthew 25:21 RSV

Catastrophe or Celebration

Worry is often linked to the fact that we don't know how to respond to past, current, or potential events in our lives, and we don't know what to do about possible consequences. We don't know whether the long-term effect of a situation will be good or bad.

A man in China raised horses for a living, and one day one of his prized stallions ran away. His friends gathered at his home to help him mourn his loss. But the next week, the horse returned, bringing with it seven strays. The same friends gathered again, this time to celebrate his good fortune. That afternoon, the horse kicked the owner's son and broke his back. The friends came again to express their sorrow and concern. But a month later, war broke out, and the man's son was exempt from military service. Again, the friends came together to rejoice.

61

Often, at the time we are going through an experience, we truly can't tell a catastrophe from a cause for celebration. God asks us to trust Him with each circumstance as it arises and walk out each day with faith. We are to expect the best, believing that God can and will work all things for good, not only in our lives, but in our students' lives as well.[14]

GOD'S Little Lessons for Teachers

Fear

My flesh and my heart may fail, But God is the strength of my heart and my portion forever.

Psalm 73:26 NASB

In the day of my trouble I will call upon You, For You will answer me.

Psalm 86:7 NKJV

Let us be bold, then, and say, "The Lord is my helper, I will not be afraid. What can anyone do to me?"

Hebrews 13:6 TEV

62

God hath not given us the spirit of fear; but of power, and of love, and of a sound mind.

2 Timothy 1:7 KJV

Leaning on the Lord

When Christian singer Sheila Walsh gave birth to her son, Christian, she was on top of the world until the physicians gave her a bad report. Her son had jaundice, which was the result of his early arrival, and a premature liver not yet able to function normally. A blood test showed something suspicious, and before Walsh knew what was happening, her son was in pediatric intensive care.

She found an empty room at the hospital and knelt down to pray. It was then that she had an inner understanding about who God really is—not a God who sends trouble to test or judge people, but a loving Father who carries our cares when times are tough. She writes in *Bring Back the Joy*, "I suddenly remembered that God had been there before me. He had watched his boy kneeling in a garden, blood flowing down his face. I knelt down broken and afraid; and when I left that room I was still afraid, but I was leaning on the Lord."

63

At times, keeping a "stiff upper lip" may be necessary to reassure your students, but with God, you never need to pretend to be brave. Bring your shattered hopes and stinging fears to Him, so He can heal you completely.[15]

GOD'S Little Lessons for Teachers

Fear

God is our refuge and strength, A very present help in trouble. Therefore we will not fear, though the earth should change, And though the mountains slip into the heart of the sea.

Psalms 46:1-2 NASB

My slanderers pursue me all day long; many are attacking me in their pride. When I am afraid, I will trust in you. In God, whose word I praise, in God I trust; I will not be afraid. What can mortal man do to me?

Psalms 56:2-4

64

That he would grant unto us, that we, being delivered out of the hand of our enemies, might serve him without fear.

Luke 1:74 KJV

Be glad for the chance to suffer as Christ suffered. It will prepare you for even greater happiness when he makes his glorious return. Count it a blessing when you suffer for being a Christian. This shows that God's glorious Spirit is with you.

1 Peter 4:13-14 CEV

Fearless Llamas

ontana rancher Lexy Lowler tried just
about everything to stop the coyotes from
killing her sheep. She used electric fences,
odor sprays, and other devices. She tried
placing battery-operated radios near them. She
tried corralling them at night and herding them by
day. She even tried sleeping with her lambs during
the summer. Even with all of her efforts, she lost
scores of lambs—fifty in one year alone!

Then Lexy tried llamas—the aggressive, funny-
looking, fearless animals generally associated with
South America. She purchased several and began
grazing them with her sheep. She said, "Llamas
don't appear to be afraid of anything. When they
see something, they put their heads up and walk
straight toward it. As far as coyotes are concerned,
such behavior is aggressive, and they won't have
anything to do with that. Coyotes are opportunists,
and llamas take that opportunity away." Not only
did Lexy solve her problem, she gained the added
benefit of llama wool spun into mohair!

Llamas intuitively seem to know the truth of
the Bible: "Resist the devil, and he will flee from
you" (James 4:7). When we are willing to resist
evil in our schools, we take an opportunity away
from the devil.[16]

65

GOD'S Little Lessons for Teachers

Forgiveness

Let the wicked leave their way of life and change their way of thinking. Let them turn to the LORD, our God; he is merciful and quick to forgive.

Isaiah 55:7 TEV

"Come now, and let us reason together," Says the LORD, "Though your sins are as scarlet, They will be as white as snow; Though they are red like crimson, They will be like wool."

Isaiah 1:18 NASB

66

Blessed is he whose transgressions are forgiven, whose sins are covered.

Psalm 32:1

Be kind to each other, tenderhearted, forgiving one another, just as God has forgiven you because you belong to Christ.

Ephesians 4:32 TLB

I'll Forgive Tonight

fter supper two little brothers were playing until bedtime. Bobby accidentally hit Joe with a stick, and Joe began to wail.
Accusations were exchanged until their exasperated mother finally sent both boys to bed.

As she tucked them in, she said, "Now, Joe, before you go to sleep, you need to forgive your brother for the mistake he made."

Joe thought for a few moments and then replied, "Well, okay. I'll forgive him tonight, but if I don't die before I wake up, he'd better look out in the morning."

67

Holding a grudge or blowing a mistake out of proportion drives a wedge between two people, and if allowed to remain, that wedge can destroy a relationship. Be quick to recognize that some mistakes are not worth mentioning and some errors are not matters of eternal importance.

Those who are quick to forgive others tend to be those who are forgiven quickly. And we all must admit, it's nice to be on the "forgiven side" of a mistake, whether we're a teacher or a student.[17]

GOD'S Little Lessons for Teachers

Forgiveness

If we confess our sins, he is faithful and just to forgive us our sins, and to cleanse us from all unrighteousness.

1 John 1:9 KJV

You, Lord, are good, and ready to forgive, And abundant in mercy to all those who call upon You.

Psalm 86:5 NKJV

68

I am the One who forgives all your sins, for my sake; I will not remember your sins.

Isaiah 43:25 NCV

If my people will humble themselves and pray, and search for me, and turn from their wicked ways, I will hear them from heaven and forgive their sins and heal their land.

2 Chronicles 7:14 TLB

Forgiving our Faults

hen it comes to forgiveness, it's sometimes easier to forgive others than to forgive ourselves. Each of the people listed below is mentioned in the Bible, and each had a fault or failing to overcome. But it did not prohibit God from using every one of them.

- Moses stuttered.
- Timothy had stomach problems.
- Jacob was a liar.
- David had an affair.
- Abraham was too old.
- John was self-righteous.
- Naomi was a poor widow.
- Paul was a murderer.
- Jonah ran from God.
- Miriam was a gossip.
- Gideon doubted—and so did Thomas.
- Jeremiah was depressed and suicidal.
- Elijah was "burned out."
- Martha was a worrywart.

69

God will forgive your faults and failings. Forgive yourself and then ask God to use you in the lives of your students and colleagues. You're just the right candidate for a job God has in mind!

GOD'S Little Lessons for Teachers

Friendship

A friend loveth at all times.

Proverbs 17:17 KJV

[Jesus said]: "No longer do I call you servants, for a servant does not know what his master is doing; but I have called you friends, for all things that I heard from My Father I have made known to you."

John 15:15 NKJV

70

Two are better than one, because they have a good return for their work: If one falls down, his friend can help him up.

Ecclesiastes 4:9-10

A man of many friends comes to ruin, But there is a friend who sticks closer than a brother.

Proverbs 18:24 NASB

Reach Out in Friendship

More than 95 percent of all Americans receive at least one Christmas card each year. The average is actually more than seventy cards per family! Millions of cards are mailed each holiday season throughout the world. Have you ever wondered where this custom originated?

A museum director in the mid-nineteenth century liked to send yearly notes to his friends at Christmas time, just to wish them a joyful holiday season. One year, he found he had little time to write, yet he still wanted to send a message of good cheer. He asked his friend John Horsely to design a card that he might sign and send. Those who received the cards loved the idea and created cards of their own. And thus, the Christmas card was invented!

71

It's often the simple, heartfelt gestures that will help you develop a rapport with your students. Ask yourself today, *What can I do to bring a smile to the face of a student? What can I do to bring good cheer into the life of a student who is needy, troubled, sick, or sorrowing?* Follow through on your inspiration, and remember, it's not a gift you are giving as much as a relationship you are building!

GOD'S Little Lessons for Teachers

Friendship

"Abraham believed God, and it was credited to him as righteousness," and he was called God's friend.

James 2:23

Wounds from a friend are better than kisses from an enemy!

Proverbs 27:6 TLB

"The greatest love you can have for your friends is to give your life for them. And you are my friends if you do what I command you."

John 15:13-14 TEV

72

The sweet smell of perfume and oils is pleasant, and so is good advice from a friend.

Proverbs 27:9 NCV

Friends Make Friends

The complex shapes of snowflakes have confounded scientists for centuries. In the past, scientists believed that the making of a snowflake was a two-step process. They believed that inside the winds of a winter storm a microscopic speck of dust would become trapped in a molecule of water vapor. Scientists suggested that this particle would then become heavily frosted with droplets of super-cooled water and plunge to earth. During its descent, the varying temperature and humidity would sculpt the heavy, icy crystal into a lacy snowflake. Or at least that's what scientists used to believe.

73

In recent decades, the true formation of the snowflake was discovered. Very few snowflakes actually contain dust or other particles. Dr. John Hallett, of the University of Nevada, discovered that the majority of snowflakes are formed from fragments of other snowflakes. As snowflakes are formed, extremely dry or cold air causes them to break up into smaller parts. The small fragments then act as seeds for new snowflakes to develop. Most of snow is made, therefore, by snow!

Teach your students that, in like manner, friendly people generate friends; their neighborly outlook inspires others to reach out and be friendly too. Instruct them to pass along the seed of friendship and watch what develops in their own lives.

GOD'S Little Lessons for Teachers

Frustration

Call to Me, and I will answer you, and show you great and mighty things, which you do not know.

Jeremiah 33:3 NKJV

We know that all things work together for good to them that love God, to them who are the called according to his purpose.

Romans 8:28 KJV

74

Encourage the exhausted, and strengthen the feeble. Say to those with anxious heart, "Take courage, fear not. Behold, your God will come."

Isaiah 35:3-4 NASB

God is faithful; he will not let you be tempted beyond what you can bear. But when you are tempted, he will also provide a way out so that you can stand up under it.

1 Corinthians 10:13

Facing the Storm

n 1992, Hurricane Andrew completely destroyed the home of one Florida couple. Devastated at the loss of all their personal belongings, the couple retreated to their vacation home on the island of Kauai to recuperate and wait for the rebuilding of their Florida home. Shortly after their arrival, a hurricane struck the Hawaiian Islands, demolishing their vacation home!

The couple acknowledged their frustration and grief in the wake of this second tragedy, but they also acknowledged God's hand on their lives. They had survived two disasters! They still had their health and human abilities. They still had faith in God and their love for one another. These were their greatest assets! They also realized that no matter where they might rebuild, their home would be vulnerable to some type of natural disaster. The point was that they must rebuild—not remain in ruins—and they must do it with optimism, not fear.

Hard times, crises, and troubles come to all of us—even teachers. It's not the nature of the crisis, but how we choose to respond to it that matters most. Those who live in faith and contentment will have the inner peace to overcome frustration and grief.[18]

75

GOD'S Little Lessons for Teachers

Frustration

The LORD says, "My thoughts are not like your thoughts. Your ways are not like my ways."

Isaiah 55:8 NCV

If God is on our side, who can ever be against us? Since he did not spare even his own Son for us but gave him up for us all, won't he also surely give us everything else?

Romans 8:31-32 TLB

76

I will make an eternal covenant with them. I will never stop doing good things for them, and I will make them fear me with all their heart, so that they will never turn away from me.

Jeremiah 32:40 TEV

Though I walk in the midst of trouble, You will revive me; You will stretch out Your hand Against the wrath of my enemies, And Your right hand will save me. The LORD will perfect that which concerns me.

Psalms 138:7-8 NKJV

Struggle of the Butterfly

A student found a cocoon one day and brought it to his biology teacher. She put it in a glass box with a warming lamp.

About a week later, the students saw a small opening appear on the cocoon. Then the cocoon began to shake. Suddenly, tiny antennae emerged, followed by a head and little front feet. The students watched the progress of the emerging insect throughout the day.

By noon it had freed its listless wings, the colors revealing it to be a monarch butterfly. It wiggled and shook, but try as it might, it did not seem to be able to force its body through the small opening. One student decided to snip off the end of the cocoon to help the insect. Out it plopped. Only the top half of it looked like a butterfly, however. The bottom half was large and swollen. The insect crawled about, dragging its listless wings, and a short time later, died.

77

The next day, the biology teacher explained that the butterfly's struggle to get through the tiny opening is necessary in order to force fluids from its swollen body into the wings so they will be strong enough to fly. Without the struggle, the wings never develop.

Teach your students to appreciate the value of personal struggle.

GOD'S Little Lessons for Teachers

Giving

He who gives to the poor will lack nothing, but he who closes his eyes to them receives many curses.

Proverbs 28:27

"Give to everyone who asks you, and if anyone takes what belongs to you, do not demand it back."

Luke 6:30

78

"Give, and it will be given to you. A good measure, pressed down, shaken together and running over, will be poured into your lap. For with the measure you use, it will be measured to you."

Luke 6:38

Each man should give what he has decided in his heart to give, not reluctantly or under compulsion, for God loves a cheerful giver.

2 Corinthians 9:7

Honeycomb Givers

 here are three kinds of givers: the flint, the sponge, and the honeycomb. Which kind are you?

To get anything from the flint, you must hammer it. Yet, all you generally get are chips and sparks. The flint gives nothing away if it can help it, and even then, only with a great display.

To get anything from the sponge, you must squeeze it. It readily yields to pressure, and the more it is pressed, the more it gives. Still, you must push.

To get anything from the honeycomb, however, you must only take what freely flows from it. It gives its sweetness generously, dripping on all without pressure, without begging or badgering.

79

Note, too, that there is another difference in the honeycomb. It is a renewable resource. Unlike the flint or sponge, the honeycomb is connected to life; it is the product of the ongoing work and creative energy of bees.

If you are a "honeycomb giver," your life will be continually replenished as you give. And, as long as you are connected to the Source of all life, you can never run dry. When you give freely to your students, you will receive in like manner, so that whatever you give away will soon be multiplied back to you.

GOD'S Little Lessons for Teachers

Giving

God did not keep back his own Son, but he gave him for us. If God did this, won't he freely give us everything else?

Romans 8:32 CEV

If I give all I possess to the poor and surrender my body to the flames, but have not love, I gain nothing.

1 Corinthians 13:3

80   In everything I did, I showed you that by this kind of hard work we must help the weak, remembering the words the Lord Jesus himself said: "It is more blessed to give than to receive."

Acts 20:35

God has given gifts to each of you from his great variety of spiritual gifts. Manage them well so that God's generosity can flow through you.

1 Peter 4:10 NLT

A Generous Spirit

Chad was a shy, quiet little boy. One day he came home and told his parents he wanted to make a valentine for everyone in his class. That night his dad and mom talked about it. Chad wasn't very popular. The other kids didn't include him in their games. He always walked home by himself. What if he went to all the trouble and then didn't receive any valentines?

They decided to encourage him anyway. Chad worked after school for three long weeks. On Valentine's Day, he excitedly put his handiwork into a paper bag and bolted out the door. Trying to be prepared for his disappointment, his parents had plans to take him out for ice cream that night.

81

After school, Chad came running home—arms empty. His folks expected him to burst into tears. "Not a one, not a one," he kept saying. His parents looked at him with wounded eyes. Then he added, "I didn't forget a single kid!"

One of the beautiful benefits of being generous toward others is that it's so rewarding, it changes the way we look at the world.

GOD'S Little Lessons for Teachers

God's Love

Now these three remain: faith, hope and love.
But the greatest of these is love.

1 Corinthians 13:13

Pursue a godly life, along with faith, love,
perseverance, and gentleness.

1 Timothy 6:11 NLT

Above all things have fervent love for one another,
for "love will cover a multitude of sins."

1 Peter 4:8 NKJV

82

Above all these put on love, which binds
everything together in perfect harmony.

Colossians 3:14 RSV

Jesus Loves Me

A minister received a call from a friend she had not seen in two years. The friend said, "My husband is leaving me for another woman. I need for you to pray with me."

The minister replied, "Come quickly."

When her friend arrived, the minister could not help but notice that she was carelessly dressed, had gained weight, and had failed to comb her hair or put on makeup. As they began to converse, the friend admitted to being an uninteresting, nagging wife and a sloppy housekeeper. The minister quickly concluded to herself, *My friend has grown to hate herself!*

83

When her friend paused to ask for her advice, the minister said only, "Will you join me in a song?" Surprised, her friend agreed. The minister began to sing, "Jesus loves me, this I know."

Her friend joined in, tears flooding her eyes. "If Jesus loves me, I must love myself, too," she concluded.

Amazing changes followed. Because she felt loved and lovable, she was transformed into the confident woman she once had been. In the process, she recaptured her husband's heart.

We can never accept God's love beyond the degree to which we are willing to love ourselves. Help your students see themselves through God's eyes. Then, it will be easier for them to fully grasp His amazing love for them.

GOD'S Little Lessons for Teachers

God's Love

"For God so loved the world that he gave his only Son, that whoever believes in him should not perish but have eternal life."

John 3:16 RSV

He will love thee, and bless thee, and multiply thee.

Deuteronomy 7:13 KJV

84

The LORD sets prisoners free, the LORD gives sight to the blind, the LORD lifts up those who are bowed down, the LORD loves the righteous.

Psalms 146:7-8

The LORD your God is with you, he is mighty to save. He will take great delight in you, he will quiet you with his love, he will rejoice over you with singing.

Zephaniah 3:17

Adopted to Belong

 Sunday school superintendent was registering two new sisters in Sunday school. She asked their ages and birthdays, so she could place them in the appropriate classes. The bolder of the two replied, "We're both seven. My birthday is April 8, and my sister's birthday is April 20."

The superintendent replied, "But that's not possible, girls."

The quieter sister spoke up. "No, it's true. One of us is adopted."

"Oh?" asked the superintendent. "Which one?"

85

The two sisters looked at each other and smiled. The bolder one said, "We asked Dad that same question awhile ago, but he just looked at us and said he loved us both equally, and he couldn't remember anymore which one of us was adopted."

What a wonderful analogy of God's love! The Apostle Paul wrote to the Romans: "Now if we are [God's] children, then we are heirs—heirs of God and co-heirs with Christ" (Romans 8:17). In essence, as adopted sons and daughters of God, we fully share in the inheritance of His only begotten Son, Jesus. Our Heavenly Father has adopted us and loves us just as much as His beloved Son.

Remember His great love for you, and pass this love on to your students!

GOD'S Little Lessons for Teachers

Gossip

Do not spread slanderous gossip among
your people.

Leviticus 19:16 NLT

The words of a whisperer are like dainty
morsels, And they go down into the innermost
parts of the body.

Proverbs 18:8 NASB

Stay away from gossips—they tell everything.

86

Proverbs 20:19 CEV

A perverse man stirs up dissension, and a gossip
separates close friends.

Proverbs 16:28

Golden Gossip

Laura Ingalls Wilder writes the following in *Little House in the Ozarks*:

I know a little band of friends that calls itself a woman's club. There is no obligation, and there are no promises; but in forming the club and in selecting new members, only those are chosen who are kind-hearted and dependable as well as the possessors of a certain degree of intelligence and a small amount of that genius which is the capacity for careful work. In short, those who are taken into membership are those who will make good friends, and so they are a little band who are each for all and all for each. . . .

87

They are getting so in the habit of speaking good words that I expect to see them all develop into Golden Gossips.

Ever hear of golden gossip? I read of it some years ago. A woman who was always talking about her friends and neighbors made it her business to talk of them, in fact, never said anything but good of them. She was a gossip, but it was "golden gossip." This woman's club seems to be working in the same way.

Teach your students the importance of only saying good things about others. Strive to turn your classroom into a Golden Gossip Club.

GOD'S Little Lessons for Teachers

Gossip

A gossip betrays a confidence, but a trustworthy man keeps a secret.

Proverbs 11:13

Where there is no wood, the fire goes out; And where there is no talebearer, strife ceases.

Proverbs 26:20 NKJV

Their words are like an open pit, and their tongues are good only for telling lies.

Romans 3:13 CEV

88

Post a guard at my mouth, GOD, set a watch at the door of my lips.

Psalm 141:3 THE MESSAGE

The Untamed Tongue

Many analogies have been given for the "untamed tongue." Quarles likened it to a drawn sword that takes a person prisoner: "A word unspoken is like the sword in the scabbard, thine; if vented, thy sword is in another's hand."

Others have compared evil speaking to the following things:

- A freezing wind—one that seals up the sparkling waters and kills the tender flowers and shoots of growth. In similar fashion, bitter and hate-filled words bind up the hearts of people and cause love to cease to flourish.
- A fox with a firebrand tied to its tail, sent out among the standing corn just as in the days of Samson and the Philistines. So gossip spreads without control or reason.
- A pistol fired in the mountains, the echo of which is intensified until it sounds like thunder.
- A snowball that gathers size as it rolls down a mountain.

Perhaps the greatest analogy, however, is one given by a little child who came running to her mother in tears. "Did your friend hurt you?" the mother asked.

"Yes," said the girl.

"Where?" asked her mother.

"Right here," said the child, pointing to her heart.

Ask God to place a watch over your tongue. Your words have the power to hurt and tear down your students, but they also have the power to heal and build them up.

GOD'S Little Lessons for Teachers

Guidance

Ask the LORD to bless your plans, and you will
be successful in carrying them out.

Proverbs 16:3 TEV

The steps of a good man are ordered by the LORD:
and he delighteth in his way.

Psalm 37:23 KJV

I am always with you; you hold me by my right
hand. You guide me with your counsel, and
afterward you will take me into glory.

Psalms 73:23-24

90

I will instruct you (says the Lord) and guide you
along the best pathway for your life; I will advise
you and watch your progress.

Psalm 32:8 TLB

God's Solution

A junior class in a Chicago church was disrupted every Sunday by one boy. The teacher was in turmoil. She asked herself, *Is my responsibility to this boy or to the others in the class who are disturbed during the lesson?*

Finally, she went to the Sunday school superintendent. He advised her that the class came first and the problem-causing boy should be told to stay home. The teacher, however, wasn't willing to settle for that solution. She felt concerned about the boy, whom she believed to be brilliant, and she could not bring herself to tell anyone to stay away from church.

91

Then she had an idea. She asked the boy to come to her house the next Saturday to help prepare some of the materials for Sunday's lesson. He gladly came without embarrassment and provided real help to her. From that time on, he often came on Saturdays. He became an asset to the class and never again was a hindrance.

Not every behavior problem can be resolved so easily, but one thing is certain: God has a solution for every problem-student. Ask the Lord to reveal the highly individualized solutions you need to reach each of your students effectively.[19]

GOD'S Little Lessons for Teachers

Guidance

This God is our God for ever and ever; he will be
our guide even to the end.

Psalm 48:14

The LORD will continually guide you, And satisfy
your desire in scorched places, And give strength to
your bones; And you will be like a watered garden,
And like a spring of water whose waters do not fail.

Isaiah 58:11 NASB

92   Trust in the LORD with all thine heart; and lean not
unto thine own understanding. In all thy ways
acknowledge him, and he shall direct thy paths.

Proverbs 3:5-6 KJV

Show me your ways, O LORD, teach me your paths;
guide me in your truth and teach me.

Psalms 25:4-5

What Did You Say?

f you ever question whether children are listening and learning from your life, consider these examples:

- A mother and her five-year-old son were driving down the street, when the little boy asked, "Mommy, why do the idiots only come out when Daddy drives?"

- After the church service, a little boy said to the pastor, "When I grow up, I'm going to give you money." "Thank you," the pastor replied, "but why?" "Because," the little boy explained, "my daddy says you're one of the poorest preachers we've ever had."

93

- A wife invited several family friends to dinner. At the table, she turned to their six-year-old daughter and said, "Would you like to say the blessing?" The girl answered, "I don't know what to say." The mother insisted, "Just say what you hear Mommy say." The daughter bowed her head and said, "Lord, why on earth did I invite all these people to dinner?"

Teachers never know when little eyes are watching their actions and little ears are hearing their words. If you want to avoid embarrassment, don't let your students hear what you don't want repeated.[20]

GOD'S Little Lessons for Teachers

Happiness

Not that I complain of want; for I have learned,
in whatever state I am, to be content.

Philippians 4:11 RSV

For to the man who pleases him God gives wisdom
and knowledge and joy.

Ecclesiastes 2:26 RSV

A glad heart makes a cheerful countenance, but
by sorrow of heart the spirit is broken.

94

Proverbs 15:13 RSV

Happiness or sadness or wealth should not keep
anyone from doing God's work.

1 Corinthians 7:30 TLB

A Beautiful Day

Barbara was having a rotten day. She had overslept and was late for work. Everything at the office had been done in a frenzy. By the time she reached the bus stop for her trip home, her stomach was in a knot. As usual, the bus was late and over-filled—she had to stand in the aisle.

A few moments after the bus pulled away, she heard a deep voice from the front of the bus say, "Beautiful day, isn't it?" She couldn't see the man, but she could hear him as he commented on the spring scenery. He called attention to each passing landmark: the church, the park, the cemetery, the firehouse. All the passengers began gazing out the windows, taking in the sight of spring foliage and late-afternoon sunshine. His enthusiasm was so contagious that even Barbara found herself smiling.

95

When the bus reached her stop, she maneuvered toward the door, glad to finally get a look at the "guide" who had brought a smile to her face. What she saw was a plump man with a black beard, wearing dark glasses and carrying a thin, white cane.

What we "see" as teachers has more to do with inner vision than physical eyesight. Choose to see those things that bring happiness to your heart.[21]

GOD'S Little Lessons for Teachers

Happiness

Happy is the man that findeth wisdom, and the man that getteth understanding

Proverbs 3:13 KJV

A generous man will himself be blessed, for he shares his food with the poor.

Proverbs 22:9

How blessed is the one whom Thou dost choose, and bring near to Thee, To dwell in Thy courts.

Psalm 65:4 NASB

96

It is possible to give freely and become more wealthy, but those who are stingy will lose everything.

Proverbs 11:24 NLT

A Bounce in His Step

r. Richard Blaylock had a first-class reputation as a competent manager and skilled clinician. When his hospital merged with another facility, however, the new administrator promptly stripped Rick of all administrative duties.

Rick felt betrayed; his ideas were ignored, and his talents were underutilized. He remained in the system five more years, but the bounce had left his step, and his usual optimism was replaced by anger and hurt. When he retired after twenty-two years of faithful service, he was not given as much as a thank you for his many contributions.

97

Rick has said, "I felt sorry for myself for about a month." Then he decided to let go of his bitterness. He heard about a rural hospital in need of a volunteer physician, and soon he was on staff—not only as a physician, but also as an administrator. Two years later, the bounce in his step was back, hospital revenues were up, good nurses had joined the staff, and the hospital was on the road to recovery.

If you feel your talents as a teacher are unappreciated and underutilized, find a place to plant them. Those who aren't sowing, aren't growing.[22]

GOD'S Little Lessons for Teachers

Honesty

Ye shall not steal, neither deal falsely, neither lie one to another.

Leviticus 19:11 KJV

That no man go beyond and defraud his brother in any matter: because that the Lord is the avenger of all such, as we also have forewarned you and testified. For God hath not called us unto uncleanness, but unto holiness.

I Thesalonians 4:6-7 KJV

98

Better a little with righteousness than much gain with injustice.

Proverbs 16:8

He that walketh righteously, and speaketh uprightly; he that despiseth the gain of oppressions, that shaketh his hands from holding of bribes, that stoppeth his ears from hearing of blood, and shutteth his eyes from seeing evil; He shall dwell on high: his place of defence shall be the munitions of rocks: bread shall be given him; his waters shall be sure.

Isaiah 33:15-16 KJV

Forty-five Seconds

Ted Engstrom tells the following story in his book titled *Integrity*:

For Coach Cleveland Stroud and the Bulldogs of Rockdale County High School (Conyers, Georgia), it was their championship season: twenty-one wins and five losses on the way to the Georgia boy's basketball tournament last March, then a dramatic come-from-behind victory in the state finals.

But now the new glass trophy case outside the high school gymnasium is bare. Earlier this month the Georgia High School Association deprived Rockdale County of the championship after school officials said that a player who was scholastically ineligible had played forty-five seconds in the first of the school's postseason games.

99

"We didn't know he was ineligible at the time; we didn't know it until a few weeks ago," Mr. Stroud said. "Some people have said we should have just kept quiet about it, that it was just forty-five seconds and the player wasn't an impact player. But you've got to do what's honest and right and what the rules say. I told my team that people forget the scores of basketball games; they don't ever forget what you're made of."

GOD'S Little Lessons for Teachers

Honesty

Lie not one to another, seeing that ye have
 put off the old man with his deeds;
And have put on the new man, which is
renewed in knowledge after the image
of him that created him.

Colossians 3:9-10 KJV

The wicked borroweth, and payeth not again:
but the righteous sheweth mercy, and giveth.

Psalm 37:21 KJV

100

Withhold not good from them to whom it is due,
when it is in the power of thine hand to do it.

Proverbs 3:27 KJV

The integrity of the upright guides them, but the
crookedness of the treacherous destroys them.

Proverbs 11:3 RSV

Senior Skip Day

 high school student announced to his mother one day, "I won't be going to school this morning."

"Are you sick?" the mother asked. "No, but it's senior skip day, and everybody will be at home."

She replied, "Everybody may skip, but you'd better be there." She knew that the assistant principal made it a priority to call about each child who didn't show up at school.

Sure enough, the assistant principal called her that evening, asking, "Is John sick?"

"No," the mother said, "I told him to be in school, and he disobeyed me."

101

The next day her son walked out of the house angry and mumbling at his long "grounding" sentence. She expected him to return home in that same mood. To her surprise, he entered the house and said, "Thank you."

"For what?" she asked.

He said, "The principal said he called parents for fourteen hours, and you were the only one who told him the truth. I think it's cool to have the only mom brave enough to tell the truth."

It takes courage to tell the truth. Kids need to learn that lesson as much as teachers need to remember it.[23]

GOD'S Little Lessons for Teachers

Hope

Behold, the eye of the LORD is upon them that fear him, upon them that hope in his mercy.

Psalm 33:18 KJV

It is good that one should hope and wait quietly For the salvation of the LORD.

Lamentations 3:26 NKJV

Happy is he whose help is the God of Jacob, whose hope is in the LORD his God.

Psalm 146:5 RSV

102

Christ has also introduced us to God's undeserved kindness on which we take our stand. So we are happy, as we look forward to sharing in the glory of God.

Romans 5:2 CEV

Is This Your Son?

A couple was about to leave their home one evening to attend an elite society party when the phone rang.

"Hello, Mom," the caller said. "I'm back in the states with an early release from my army duties in Vietnam!"

"Wonderful!" the mother exclaimed. "When will you be home?"

"I'd like to bring a buddy home with me," the son replied. "Both of his legs have been amputated, one arm is gone, his face is disfigured, and one ear and one eye are missing. He's not much to look at, but he needs a home real bad."

"Sure, bring him home for a few days," she said.

103

"You don't understand," the young man said, "I want to bring him home to live there with you."

The mother stammered, "What would our friends think? It would be too much for your father. . . ." Before she could finish, she heard a dial tone.

Later that night when the couple returned home, they had a message to call the police department. The chief of police said, "Ma'am, we just found a young man with both legs and one arm missing. His face is badly mangled. He has taken his life, and his identification indicates he is your son."

All of your students need love and acceptance, especially those who face special challenges. Build up their hopes, and support their dreams. In doing so, your own hopes as a teacher will be strengthened as well.[24]

GOD'S Little Lessons for Teachers

Hope

Praise be to the God and Father of our Lord Jesus Christ! In his great mercy he has given us new birth into a living hope through the resurrection of Jesus Christ from the dead, and into an inheritance that can never perish, spoil or fade— kept in heaven for you.

1 Peter 1:3-4

O Lord, you alone are my hope. I've trusted you, O LORD, from childhood.

Psalm 71:5 NLT

104

When they see me waiting, expecting your Word, those who fear you will take heart and be glad.

Psalm 119:74 THE MESSAGE

Hope in God and wait expectantly for Him, for I shall yet praise Him, my Help and my God.

Psalm 42:5 AMP

Big Plans

esearchers at Wright Patterson Air Force Base have been working on a project called "brain-actuated control." They are hoping to develop a means for pilots to fly airplanes with their minds.

In their experiments, the pilots wear scalp monitors that pick up electrical signals from various points in the brain. The scalp monitors are wired to a computer. Using biofeedback techniques, the pilots are able to direct the electrical activity created by their own thought processes. The computer then translates the electrical signals into mechanical commands for the airplane.

105

Although controlling airplanes with the mind is yet to be perfected, the mind certainly has tremendous control over one thing—behavior. Eventually, thoughts erupt into actions. The height of our success only has one major ceiling: the height of our dreams.

One prisoner knew this. Suspended in a spread-eagled position, secured by manacles and chains above the damp floor of a dungeon, he looked up about forty feet to the only window in the cell. Immobile and pinned to the wall, he said to the other prisoner in his dungeon cell, "Here's my plan!"

God-given dreams are always big. Choose to dream them on behalf of yourself and your students.[25]

GOD'S Little Lessons for Teachers

Joy

For ye shall go out with joy, and be led forth with peace: the mountains and the hills shall break forth before you into singing, and all the trees of the field shall clap their hands.

Isaiah 55:12 KJV

Blessed is the people that know the joyful sound: they shall walk, O LORD, in the light of thy countenance. In thy name shall they rejoice all the day: and in thy righteousness shall they be exalted.

Psalms 89:15-16 KJV

106

The voice of rejoicing and salvation is in the tabernacles of the righteous: the right hand of the LORD doeth valiantly.

Psalm 118:15 KJV

"These things have I spoken unto you, that my joy might remain in you, and that your joy might be full."

John 15:11 KJV

Life's Little Joys

Each day, a man routinely walked to and from his office along Lake Michigan—a beautiful way to combine his commute to work with exercise. He enjoyed the walk on most days but was frustrated by the automated sprinkler systems along the walkway. Specifically, he found it annoying that the sprinklers sprayed water beyond the lawns onto the sidewalks.

One day as he swerved to avoid the sweep of a sprinkler, he noticed a woman jogging past him. She headed straight for the sprinkler. When she reached it, she simply stopped in her tracks, her Walkman still clamped to her ears, and let the sprinkler soak her completely. The executive found himself chuckling inside at the obvious joy she took in being sprayed by the sprinkler. He noticed that several others also were smiling, obviously enjoying the freedom she seemed to experience. Reflecting on this as he continued his walk, the executive concluded the jogger had found a way to appreciate the little joys in life rather than becoming mad, sad, or afraid. He found himself interested in wanting to know why.

107

Today, respond to everything you experience with joy and delight. A joyful response to life is one of the greatest witnesses a teacher can have![26]

GOD'S Little Lessons for Teachers

Joy

Thou hast put gladness in my heart, more than in the time that their corn and their wine increased.

Psalm 4:7 KJV

They that sow in tears shall reap in joy. He that goeth forth and weepeth, bearing precious seed, shall doubtless come again with rejoicing, bringing his sheaves with him.

Psalms 126:5-6 KJV

108   Yet I will rejoice in the LORD, I will joy in the God of my salvation.

Habakkuk 3:18 KJV

For our heart shall rejoice in him, because we have trusted in his holy name.

Psalm 33:21 KJV

A Responsibility and a Privilege

George Mueller would not preach until his heart was "happy in the grace of God."

Jan Ruybroeck would not write while his feelings were low; he would retire to a quiet place and wait on God until he felt joy in his heart.

It was the happy laughter and joy of a group of Moravian Christians that convinced John Wesley of the reality of their faith and helped bring him to a point of genuine spiritual conversion.

Joy is both the responsibility and the privilege of every Christian. As Henry Evansen wrote:

109

- It costs nothing, but creates much.
- It enriches those who receive it without impoverishing those who give it.
- It happens in a flash, and the memory of it sometimes lasts forever.
- None are so rich that they can get along without it, and none so poor but are richer for its benefits.
- It fosters good will in a business, creates happiness in a home, and is the countersign of friends. It is rest to the weary, daylight to the discouraged, sunshine to the sad, and nature's best antidote for trouble.

What is it? A smile!

Teach with a smile and a happy heart today![27]

GOD'S Little Lessons for Teachers

Knowledge

Praise God forever and ever, because he has wisdom and power. . . . He gives wisdom to those who are wise and knowledge to those who understand.

Daniel 2:20-21 NCV

Wisdom and knowledge will be the stability of your times, And the strength of salvation.

Isaiah 33:6 NKJV

110 O the depth of the riches both of the wisdom and knowledge of God! how unsearchable are his judgments, and his ways past finding out!

Romans 11:33 KJV

Wisdom will enter your heart, And knowledge will be pleasant to your soul.

Proverbs 2:10 NASB

Follow the Hawk

n an issue of *Guideposts,* Ronald Pinkerton describes a near accident he had while hang gliding. As he descended, a powerful blast of air hit his hang glider, plummeting him toward the ground.

He wrote:

I was falling at an alarming rate. Trapped in an airborne riptide, I was going to crash! Then I saw him—a red-tailed hawk. He was six feet off my right wingtip, fighting the same gust I was . . . suddenly he banked and flew straight downwind. If the right air is anywhere, it's upwind! The hawk was committing suicide. . . .

111

From nowhere the thought entered my mind: *Follow the hawk.* It went against everything I knew about flying. But now all my knowledge was useless. I followed the hawk. . . . Suddenly the hawk gained altitude. Then a warm surge of air started pushing the glider upward. I was stunned. Nothing I knew as a pilot could explain this phenomenon. But it was true: I was rising.

From time to time, each of us is forced to admit we don't know what to do. Look around. God has placed somebody in your path to be your teacher in those moments. Choose to learn from that person.[28]

GOD'S Little Lessons for Teachers

Knowledge

A man of understanding and knowledge
maintains order.

Proverbs 28:2

The fear of the LORD is the beginning of wisdom,
and knowledge of the Holy One is understanding.

Proverbs 9:10

If I have the gift of prophecy and can fathom
all mysteries and all knowledge, and if I have
a faith that can move mountains, but have
not love, I am nothing.

1 Corinthians 13:2

112

Grow in the grace and knowledge of our Lord
and Savior Jesus Christ.

2 Peter 3:18 NASB

Missing Pages

n *True Success,* Tom Morris writes, "A setback is not always bad." Morris learned this from personal experience. He lost several pages of his book after writing them out in longhand. For three days, he looked everywhere for them, both at home and at work. The search took up valuable writing time and produced little except unrelated items he had forgotten about.

A friend heard about Morris's problem and took it upon himself to search through a large, full dumpster outside his office building. He dug through mounds of refuse and paper, and within a couple of hours he knocked at Morris's office door and produced slightly wrinkled and "aromatic" sheets of paper. They were the lost pages!

Morris writes of the experience, "I learned some lessons and gained some insights I would have missed if things had gone smoothly and I never had lost those pages. Lessons that have helped me with my book. Insights that have helped me with my life." Ironically, the pages that Morris had lost were pages from a chapter in his book on "setbacks and detours!"

A wise teacher never stops learning from as many sources as possible.[29]

GOD'S Little Lessons for Teachers

Laughter

There is a time for everything, and a season for every activity under heaven: . . . a time to weep and a time to laugh, a time to mourn and a time to dance.

Ecclesiastes 3:1,4

He will yet fill your mouth with laughter and your lips with shouts of joy.

Job 8:21

114

Our mouths were filled with laughter, our tongues with songs of joy.

Psalm 126:2

"Blessed are you who hunger now, for you will be satisfied. Blessed are you who weep now, for you will laugh."

Luke 6:21

The Laugh Cure

r. Fry has called laughter a stationary jogger. He has said, "There is hardly a system in the body a hearty laugh doesn't stimulate."

Norman Cousins, former editor of *Saturday Review,* believed that his recovery from a deadly form of spinal arthritis was due to massive doses of vitamin C and a tremendous amount of laughter every day. More than seventy years ago, Bernard MacFadden wrote that laughter is a form of exercise. He and his followers derived so much benefit from laughter exercise that he called it his "Laugh Cure."

115

Laughter has long been regarded as a sign of mental health. In the recent movie *Patch Adams,* Dr. Hunter Adams, while still a medical student, gives a long list of laughter's benefits to a supervising physician, benefits which inlude a greater release of endorphins and other hormones to the brain, relaxed muscle systems, increased circulation, and lower blood pressure.

Choosing to have fun and laugh heartily at life's foibles may be one of the best choices a teacher can make for health and genuine quality of life. It certainly is worth a try, since laughter has no known negative side effects![30]

GOD'S Little Lessons for Teachers

Loneliness

Turn to me and be gracious to me, For I am lonely and afflicted.

Psalm 25:16 NASB

Even if my father and mother abandon me, the LORD will hold me close.

Psalm 27:10 NLT

116

"Though the mountains be shaken and the hills be removed, yet my unfailing love for you will not be shaken nor my covenant of peace be removed," says the LORD, who has compassion on you.

Isaiah 54:10

The eternal God is thy refuge, and underneath are the everlasting arms.

Deuteronomy 33:27 KJV

Learning from Isolation

On July 22, 1996, a Japanese teenager set out in a thirty-foot yacht on a solo voyage across the Pacific Ocean. On September 13, fourteen-year-old Subaru Takahashi sailed under the Golden Gate Bridge—the youngest person in recorded history to make the 4,600-mile journey alone. Midway into his journey, the motor on his yacht quit. His battery died five days later. Amazingly, Takahashi made the last 2,790 miles of his trip under "sail" power alone.

To prepare for this trip, Takahashi spent five hundred hours of intensive training with yachting experts. Yet this was not his first solo voyage. He began canoeing at age five and crossed the nineteen-mile Sado Strait in the Sea of Japan in a solo canoe when he was only nine years old.

117

One of the challenges of a solo sailor's long voyage is the feeling of isolation. Rather than bemoan the loneliness of his venture, Takahashi made solitude his ally, marking the days with a deeper awareness of his abilities and a greater respect for creation. Solitude ultimately warmed his soul and strengthened his resolve.

Learn to use your time alone as a time for growth. This positive approach will keep you focused and help you achieve your goals as well.

GOD'S Little Lessons for Teachers

Loneliness

"Don't be troubled. You trust God, now trust in me."

John 14:1 NLT

He heals the brokenhearted And binds up their wounds.

Psalm 147:3 NKJV

Since we are all one body in Christ, we belong to each other, and each of us needs all the others.

118

Romans 12:5 NLT

God makes a home for the lonely; He leads out the prisoners into prosperity, Only the rebellious dwell in a parched land.

Psalm 68:6 NASB

Overcoming Loneliness

naffectionate and uncaring, Mary Lennox had no concept of what life was like outside of India. Largely ignored by her parents and raised by servants, Mary always insisted on having her own way and refused to share her things with other children.

When Mary was nine years old, her parents died of cholera. She was sent to live at her uncle's home in England. The move, however, did nothing to improve her disposition. She still expected everyone to jump at her commands.

Gradually, however, Mary began to change. In her loneliness, she asked a robin in the garden to be her friend. She began to treat her maid with more respect and even began to crave the approval of her maid's little brother, Dickon. Mary began to seek his advice on things and even revealed to him the location of her own little garden. Eventually, she convinced her crippled cousin, Colin, to grab hold of life with both hands. By the last page of *The Secret Garden*, Mary's transformation is complete. She is happy with herself and surrounded by friends, and her loneliness is but a distant memory.

Teach your students that to make friends, they first must prove themselves to be friendly.

119

GOD'S Little Lessons for Teachers

Love

The fruit of the Spirit is love, joy, peace, long-suffering, gentleness, goodness, faith.

Galatians 5:22 KJV

Above all, love each other deeply, because love covers over a multitude of sins.

1 Peter 4:8

120

Whoever loves is a child of God and knows God. Whoever does not love does not know God, for God is love.

1 John 4:7-8 TEV

I have loved you with an everlasting love; Therefore I have drawn you with lovingkindness.

Jeremiah 31:3 NASB

A Brother's Gift

A man named Paul once received a new car as a gift from his wealthy brother. One evening as Paul was leaving work, he noticed a poor child eyeing his shiny new car. "Is this your car?" the boy asked.

Paul nodded and said, "My brother gave it to me for Christmas."

The boy said, "It didn't cost you nothing? Boy, I wish. . . ." Paul expected the boy to wish that he had a generous brother, but what the boy said astonished him. He said, "I wish I could be a brother like that."

He asked the boy if he'd like a ride home. The little boy hopped in quickly. Paul smiled, figuring that the boy was eager to show off to his neighbors and family. Again, he was wrong. When the two pulled up in front of the boy's house, the boy asked Paul to wait a minute. He then ran up the steps and soon returned carrying his crippled brother. Paul was moved deeply when he heard him say, "There it is, Buddy, just like I told you upstairs. His brother gave it to him. Someday I'm gonna give you one just like it."

Generosity is a vital aspect of friendship and community—in a school as well as a church. When you give to your students, you are demonstrating your love for them in a practical way, so choose to be a giver. Joy will be the result, not only in your students' hearts, but in your own heart as well.[31]

121

GOD'S Little Lessons for Teachers

Love

We need have no fear of someone who loves us perfectly; his perfect love for us eliminates all dread.

1 John 4:18 TLB

"Love your enemies, do good, and lend, hoping for nothing in return; and your reward will be great."

Luke 6:35 NKJV

"This is my commandment, That ye love one another, as I have loved you."

John 15:12 KJV

122

Those who do not love their brothers and sisters, whom they have seen, cannot love God, whom they have never seen.

1 John 4:20 NCV

A Jar of Flowers

 ew physicians make house calls these days, but one doctor decided to do so, believing that his patient would do better if she could be treated in the comfort of her own home. Cancer was causing fluid to build up in her lung, and this fluid needed to be drained periodically.

At each visit, the physician spent time talking with the woman about subjects that were of interest to her. One day after finishing his procedure, he commented on the beautiful flowers just outside her window. She said to him, "Those flowers are one of the reasons my home is so dear to me. It gives me great joy to look out the window and see them."

123

A short time later, the woman died. Her daughter came to the physician's office one day with a gift from his former patient—a jar filled with beautiful flowers from the woman's garden. The note with the flowers read: "It was my mother's desire to share with you some of the beauty you made possible for her to hang onto in her last days. Thank you for everything."

Who was the more loving? The sick woman no doubt thought the physician was—the physician had no doubt that his patient and her daughter were.

Love keeps on giving. Its message is an eternal one that no student or colleague tires of hearing.[32]

GOD'S Little Lessons for Teachers

Money/Materialism

The love of money is a root of all kinds of evil, for which some have strayed from the faith in their greediness, and pierced themselves through with many sorrows.

1 Timothy 6:10 NKJV

Give me an eagerness for your decrees; do not inflict me with love for money!

Psalm 119:36 NLT

124   Wisdom is a shelter as money is a shelter, but the advantage of knowledge is this: that wisdom preserves the life of its possessor.

Ecclesiastes 7:12

Instruct those who are rich in this present world not to be conceited or to fix their hope on the uncertainty of riches, but on God, who richly supplies us with all things to enjoy.

1 Timothy 6:17 NASB

Money, Money, Money

n 1923, eight of the most powerful money magnates in the world gathered for a meeting at the Edgewater Beach Hotel in Chicago, Illinois. The combined resources and assets of these eight men tallied more than the United States Treasury that year. In the group were: Charles Schwab, president of a steel company; Richard Whitney, president of the New York Stock Exchange; Arthur Cutton, a wheat speculator; Albert Fall, a presidential cabinet member and personally wealthy man; Jesse Livermore, the greatest Wall Street "bear" in his generation; Leon Fraser, the president of the International Bank of Settlements; and Ivan Krueger, head of the largest monopoly in the nation. Together they made up quite an impressive gathering of financial eagles!

125

What happened to these men in later years? Schwab died penniless. Whitney served a life sentence in Sing Sing prison. Cutton became insolvent. Fall was pardoned from a federal prison so he might die at home. Fraser, Livermore, and Krueger committed suicide. Seven of these eight extremely rich men ended their lives with nothing.

Money is certainly not the answer to life's ills! Only God can give us peace, happiness, and joy. When we focus on God and His goodness, we can live contentedly, knowing that He will meet all our needs.

GOD'S Little Lessons for Teachers

Money/Materialism

"Don't store up treasures here on earth where they can erode away or may be stolen. Store them in heaven where they will never lose their value."

Matthew 6:19-20 TLB

Stay away from the love of money; be satisfied with what you have.

Hebrews 13:5 NLT

126

"Be careful and guard against all kinds of greed. Life is not measured by how much one owns."

Luke 12:15 NCV

"No one can serve two masters. Either he will hate the one and love the other, or he will be devoted to the one and despise the other. You cannot serve both God and Money."

Matthew 6:24

A Fitting Monument

 strange group of gravestones stands in Mt. Hope Cemetery in Hiawatha, Kansas. A man named Davis had them made. When his wife died, Davis erected an elaborate statue in her memory. It showed both her and him at opposite ends of a love seat. He was so pleased with the result, he commissioned another statue, this time of himself placing a wreath as he kneeled at her grave. He was so impressed by this one that he had a third monument made, one of his wife— now with angel wings on her back—placing a wreath at his future grave. One idea led to another, and in the end he spent more than a quarter million dollars on monuments to himself and his wife.

127

Meanwhile, any townsperson who approached Davis concerning financial help for a worthy community project—such as a hospital or park— was quickly silenced. The old miser would frown, set his jaw, and shout back, "What's this town ever done for me? I don't owe this town nuthin'!"

John Davis died at ninety-two, a lonely and bitter resident of the "poorhouse." Few attended his funeral. And the monuments? Each is sinking into the Kansas soil because of time, vandalism, and neglect.

As a teacher, choose to carve your legacy on young hearts, rather than stone, and you will receive an eternal reward for your efforts.[33]

GOD'S Little Lessons for Teachers

Patience

Be patient and wait for the LORD to act; don't be worried about those who prosper or those who succeed in their evil plans.

Psalm 37:47 TEV

It is better to be patient than to be proud. Don't become angry quickly, because getting angry is foolish.

Ecclesiastes 7:8-9 NCV

128   When the Holy Spirit controls our lives he will produce this kind of fruit in us: love, joy, peace, patience, kindness, goodness, faithfulness.

Galatians 5:22 TLB

Be completely humble and gentle; be patient, bearing with one another in love.

Ephesians 4:2

Options

T he last place most people want to be is stuck on an ice-covered road in a traffic jam. Bill found himself in just that position at the base of an icy hill one morning. He knew there was no hope except to turn around slowly. He maneuvered his vehicle off the pavement and onto the grassy shoulder where he thought he could gain more traction to turn his car around. *Patience, Bill,* he kept telling himself. It took him ten slow, frustrating minutes, but he finally was able to turn around. Then, suddenly a car came up too quickly behind him, skidded on the ice, and crashed at a ninety-degree angle into the truck immediately in front of him. He was trapped again—this time by an accident!

129

After checking to make certain both drivers were uninjured, Bill used his cell phone to call for a tow truck. *Why didn't I think of using my car phone earlier?* he asked himself. For the next hour, Bill made phone calls—the same calls he would have made at his desk in the office. He accomplished an entire morning's work by the side of an icy road.

When delays come your way, trust God for two things a teacher needs every day: patience and options. Then ask Him for the creativity to utilize every tool He has given you.

GOD'S Little Lessons for Teachers

Patience

I waited patiently for the LORD to help me, and he turned to me and heard my cry.

Psalm 40:1 NLT

Let us lay aside every weight, and the sin which doth so easily beset us, and let us run with patience the race that is set before us.

Hebrews 12:1 KJV

130

Warn those who are unruly, comfort the fainthearted, uphold the weak, be patient with all.

1 Thessalonians 5:14 NKJV

The Lord is not slow about His promise, as some count slowness, but is patient toward you, not wishing for any to perish but for all to come to repentance.

2 Peter 3:9 NASB

I Can Hold Myself

Danny's world was turned upside down when his father died—his home totally changed, and his mother became ill. Although his loved ones understood the reason for his insecurity, they didn't know how to deal with his tirades. A special teacher was consulted.

The teacher spent some time with Danny, and when he went into one of his "cyclone imitations," she quietly, but firmly, took hold of his arms and looked him steadily in the eyes. He looked back in fear, expecting her to punish him. Instead she said, "Danny, when little boys act that way, I hold them like this until they get quiet inside."

131

He didn't struggle. After a moment he said, "You can let go now. I won't do it again."

The teacher said, "Fine," and she let go.

The next day, Danny started on a rampage again, this time with one eye on his teacher. She walked slowly toward him, as she had the day before, but before she reached him, he suddenly grabbed his own arms and said, "You don't have to hold me. I can hold myself." And he did.

Eventually, your students must learn to discipline themselves. It helps, however, to have a patient teacher who shows by example how to hold with arms of love.[34]

GOD'S Little Lessons for Teachers

Peace

Great peace have they who love your law, and
nothing can make them stumble.

Psalm 119:165

LORD, Thou wilt establish peace for us, Since
Thou hast also performed for us all our works.

Isaiah 26:12 NASB

132

Be perfect, be of good comfort, be of one mind,
live in peace; and the God of love and peace
shall be with you.

2 Corinthians 13:11 KJV

When a man's ways are pleasing to the LORD, He
makes even his enemies to be at peace with him.

Proverbs 16:7 NASB

A Battle of Wills

An extreme example of an adult acting like a child is portrayed in the movie *Mommie Dearest,* based upon a book by Christina Crawford. In one scene, the mother insists that her daughter finish eating a piece of steak on her plate. The daughter refuses, insisting that the meat is raw.

Long after the rest of the family has left the table, the daughter is forced by her mother to remain there. The mother is determined to win this battle of wills. The daughter falls asleep at the table, only to find the piece of steak on her breakfast plate the next morning. The battle continues for several meals, the piece of meat appearing on each plate put before the child until finally the mother gives in and disposes of the offensive, rotting meat.

133

What lesson does the daughter learn in this? Sadly, she seemed only to learn that adults can be as stubborn as children.

Are you in a contest of wills with a student today? Is eternity at stake? Is evil truly afoot? Or are you simply engaged in a battle to save face or to determine who is more powerful? Those who seek peace—and use peaceful means to reach it—are generally the winners in the long run.

GOD'S Little Lessons for Teachers

Peace

Turn your back on sin; do something good.
Embrace peace—don't let it get away!

Psalm 34:14 THE MESSAGE

Therefore, since we have been made right in God's
sight by faith, we have peace with God because of
what Jesus Christ our Lord has done for us.

Romans 5:1 NLT

134

May the God of hope fill you with all joy and peace
as you trust in him, so that you may overflow
with hope by the power of the Holy Spirit.

Romans 15:13

The meek shall inherit the earth; and shall delight
themselves in the abundance of peace.

Psalm 37:11 KJV

No Hard Feelings

ecently, martial arts expert and actor Chuck Norris went into a Texas cafe and sat down to order something cool to drink. A large man approached the booth, towered over him, and notified him that he was sitting in his booth. Norris liked neither the man's tone nor his implied threat, but he said nothing. He just moved to another booth.

A few minutes later, the man moved in his direction. Norris thought, *Here it comes. A local tough out to make a name for himself by taking on Chuck Norris in a fight.* This time, however, the man said, "You're Chuck Norris." Norris nodded, and the man continued, "You could have whipped me back there a few minutes ago. Why didn't you?"

135

Norris replied, "What would it have proven?"

The man thought for a moment and then extended his hand. "No hard feelings?" he asked.

"None," Norris responded and shook his hand. He had won a confrontation, not by a display of martial arts, but by losing his seat in a cafe. And in the process he had also made a new friend.

What are you willing to lose in order to gain your students' respect and God's approval and reward?[35]

GOD'S Little Lessons for Teachers

Perseverance

Consider it pure joy, my brothers, whenever you face trials of many kinds, because you know that the testing of your faith develops perseverance. Perseverance must finish its work so that you may be mature and complete, not lacking anything.
James 1:2-4

May the Master take you by the hand and lead you along the path of God's love and Christ's endurance.
2 Thessalonians 3:5 THE MESSAGE

136

Love bears up under anything and everything that comes, is ever ready to believe the best of every person, its hopes are fadeless under all circumstances, and it endures everything [without weakening].
1 Corinthians 13:7 AMP

If anyone suffers as a Christian, let him not feel ashamed, but in that name let him glorify God.
1 Peter 4:16 NASB

Dream Big

ictor Villasenor remained illiterate until adulthood because of dyslexia. Then a woman in his native country of Mexico taught him to read. Ironically, Victor decided he wanted to become a great writer and asked God to help him fulfill his dream.

For ten years, Victor worked hard at manual labor, digging ditches and cleaning houses. As he worked, he thought of interesting characters and plots. At night, he read voraciously, devouring more than five-thousand books, memorizing favorite opening lines, and analyzing literary styles. Then he started writing: nine novels, sixty-five short stories, and ten plays. He sent them all to publishers—and all were rejected. One publisher sent a two-word response: "You're kidding."

137

Instead of being discouraged, Victor was happy that the publisher had read his work! In 1972, after 260 rejections, Victor sold his first novel, *Macho*. He then published a nonfiction book and an award-winning screenplay. He is best known for his saga about his own family, *Rain of Gold*, which took twelve years to write.

Encourage your students to dream big! Then motivate them to turn those dreams into reality![36]

GOD'S Little Lessons for Teachers

Perseverance

We also glory in tribulations, knowing that tribulation produces perseverance; and perseverance, character; and character, hope.

Romans 5:3-4 NKJV

You need to persevere so that when you have done the will of God, you will receive what he has promised.

Hebrews 10:36

138   "The good soil represents honest, good-hearted people who hear God's message, cling to it, and steadily produce a huge harvest."

Luke 8:15 NLT

Pray at all times in the Spirit, with all prayer and supplication. To that end keep alert with all perseverance, making supplication for all the saints.

Ephesians 6:18 RSV

Twenty-seven Seconds

The movie *Rudy* is based upon the life of Daniel E. Ruettiger. Rudy grew up listening to legends about Notre Dame football. He dreamed of playing there one day, but friends advised him that he was neither a good enough student to be admitted to the university nor a good enough athlete to make the team. So Rudy went to work in a power plant.

Then a friend of his was killed in an accident at work. Shaken, Rudy realized that life is too short not to pursue his dreams. At the age of twenty-three, he enrolled at Holy Cross Junior College. He made good enough grades to transfer to Notre Dame and worked until he made the football squad as part of the scout team—players who help the varsity prepare and practice but who never suit up for the games.

139

The coach allowed Rudy to suit up for the final game of his senior year. In the final minutes of the game, a student in the stands began yelling, "We want Rudy!" Others joined in. With only twenty-seven seconds left on the game clock, Rudy took the field—and made the final tackle. He had persisted until he reached his goal.

Never give up on a student. A goal is worth pursuing until it is reached.[37]

GOD'S Little Lessons for Teachers

Prayer

"When you pray, go away by yourself, all alone, and shut the door behind you and pray to your Father secretly, and your Father, who knows your secrets, will reward you."

Matthew 6:6 TLB

Even before they finish praying to me, I will answer their prayers.

Isaiah 65:24 TEV

140

"Believe that you have received the things you ask for in prayer, and God will give them to you."

Mark 11:24 NCV

The earnest prayer of a righteous person has great power and wonderful results.

James 5:16 NLT

A Drowning Man

n *The Wonderful Spirit-Filled Life,* Charles Stanley writes:

> In water-safety courses a cardinal rule is never to swim out to a drowning man and try to help him as long as he is thrashing about. To do so is to commit suicide. As long as a drowning man thinks he can help himself, he is dangerous to anyone who tries to help him. His tendency is to grab the one trying to aid him and take them both down in the process.

> The correct procedure is to stay just far enough away so that he can't grab you. Then you wait. And when he finally gives up, you make your move. At that point the one drowning is pliable. He won't work against you. He will let you help.

141

It is wise to pray, *I can't do this job with my own strength and ability. I need You, God. Please help me know what is right and best for the children that You have entrusted to my care.* Such a prayer puts a teacher into the best possible position to receive help from the Master Teacher—the One who knows all the questions, all the solutions, and all the answers for all of eternity![38]

GOD'S Little Lessons for Teachers

Prayer

The eyes of the Lord watch over those who do
right, and his ears are open to their prayers.

1 Peter 3:12 NLT

"When you are praying, if you are angry with
someone, forgive him so that your Father in
heaven will also forgive your sins."

Mark 11:25 NCV

142   Call unto me, and I will answer thee, and
show thee great and mighty things, which
thou knowest not.

Jeremiah 33:3 KJV

When good people pray, the LORD listens.

Proverbs 15:29 TEV

Prayer Paves the Path

ohn Burrill has written, "I do a full day of work in the office, run a six-room house with two active sons, and consider it easy. My wife has been ill for years, but my house could stand a 'white-glove' inspection any Sunday afternoon. I also have found time to canvass neighbors in support of a school bond issue and serve as treasurer of a Boy Scout troop and a P.T.A. committeeman."

Burrill's secrets: "Two fine sons and organization, partly. But the real answer is that we three take time every day for prayer. God does the rest. If everybody would spend a few minutes daily in quiet self-inspection and rearrangement of real values, homes would be homes: places where each member of the family gathers strength for the next day."

143

Paul Yongi Cho, pastor of the world's largest church in Seoul, South Korea, once noted, "The more I have to do, the more appointments and the more decisions I have to make, and the greater the responsibility God gives to me for others, the more I have to pray. When the church was smaller, I only prayed an hour a day. Now I pray three hours."

Prayer paves the path God asks us to take, including the path down the hall to a classroom.[39]

GOD'S Little Lessons for Teachers

Priorities

Seek the LORD and his strength, seek his presence continually! Remember the wonderful works that he has done, the wonders he wrought.

1 Chronicles 16:11-12 RSV

Let the word of Christ dwell in you richly in all wisdom; teaching and admonishing one another in psalms and hymns and spiritual songs, singing with grace in your hearts to the Lord. And whatsoever ye do in word or deed, do all in the name of the Lord Jesus, giving thanks to God and the Father by him.

Colossians 3:16-17 KJV

144

GOD, my God! How I search for you! How I thirst for you in this parched and weary land where there is no water. How I long to find you! At last I shall be fully satisfied; I will praise you with great joy.

Psalms 63:1,5 TLB

"What good will it be for a man if he gains the whole world, yet forfeits his soul?"

Matthew 16:26

The Gift of Life

nce a nationally syndicated columnist and now an author, Anna Quindlen seems to have enjoyed success at everything she has attempted. However, in taking a fellow commentator to task after he made light of teenage problems, Anna was reminded of the two attempts she had made to end her own life at age sixteen. She writes, "I was really driven through my high school years. I always had to be perfect in every way, ranging from how I looked to how my grades were. It was too much pressure."

In the early 1970s, Anna's mother died from ovarian cancer. This tragedy cured Anna from any desire to commit suicide. Her attitude toward life changed. "I could never look at life as anything but a great gift. I realized I didn't have any business taking it for granted."

145

When we are faced with the realization that life is temporary, we can finally come to grips with what is important. When we face our own immortality, our priorities quickly come into focus.

Consider your life as God's gift to you. Every moment is precious, so cherish them all. In doing so, you'll find purpose and meaning for each day you spend in your classroom.

GOD'S Little Lessons for Teachers

Priorities

"If any man will come after me, let him deny himself, and take up his cross daily, and follow me. For whosoever will save his life shall lose it: but whosoever will lose his life for my sake, the same shall save it. For what is a man advantaged, if he gain the whole world, and lose himself, or be cast away?"

Luke 9:23-25 KJV

Speak to one another with psalms, hymns and spiritual songs. Sing and make music in your heart to the Lord, always giving thanks to God the Father for everything, in the name of our Lord Jesus Christ.

Ephesians 5:19-20

146

By him therefore let us offer the sacrifice of praise to God continually, that is, the fruit of our lips, giving thanks to his name.

Hebrews 13:15 KJV

I appeal to you therefore, brethren, by the mercies of God, to present your bodies as a living sacrifice, holy and acceptable to God, which is your spiritual worship.

Romans 12:1 RSV

To Please the Master

A young man once studied violin under a world-renowned violinist. He worked hard for several years perfecting his talent, and the day finally came when he was called upon to give his first major public recital in the large city where both he and his teacher lived. Following each selection, which he performed with great skill and passion, the performer seemed uneasy about the tremendous applause he received. Even though he knew those in the audience were musically astute and not likely to give such applause to a less than superior performance, the young man acted almost as if he couldn't hear the appreciation that was being showered upon him.

147

At the close of the last number, the applause was thunderous, and numerous "Bravos" were shouted. The talented young violinist, however, had his eyes glued on only one spot. Finally, when an elderly man in the first row of the balcony smiled and nodded to him in approval, the young man relaxed and beamed with both relief and joy. His teacher had praised his work! The applause of thousands meant nothing until he had first won the approval of the master. His top priority was to please his teacher.

Whom are you most trying to please today? Remember to keep your eyes on your Heavenly Master and seek His approval only.

Renewal

Do not conform any longer to the pattern of this world, but be transformed by the renewing of your mind. Then you will be able to test and approve what God's will is—his good, pleasing and perfect will.

Romans 12:2

Create in me a clean heart, O God; and renew a right spirit within me.

Psalm 51:10 KJV

148

Therefore if any man be in Christ, he is a new creature: old things are passed away; behold, all things are become new.

2 Corinthians 5:17 KJV

I will seek that which was lost, and bring again that which was driven away, and will bind up that which was broken, and will strengthen that which was sick.

Ezekiel 34:16 KJV

Transformation

wo friends who were both in love with men who had serious problems, decided to meet weekly to fast and pray. Over the weeks and months that followed, they prayed for every possible "angle" related to the difficulties their loved ones were experiencing. One of the women said, "We were praying for a *total* healing in their lives. Looking back, I realize we were also asking God to transform them into the men we thought they should be, and which we genuinely thought God wanted them to be."

After nearly a year, both of the women thought they had prayed all they could. "Nothing happened to improve our relationships," one of the women said. "Both men went their own way, and we know of no change in their attitudes or behavior. What *did* happen was that my friend and I were transformed. We were healed of broken hearts and shattered dreams. We had our faith renewed and our hope restored. God surely will work in their lives, but the real miracle happened in us!"

149

When you pray for change in your students, you may not get what you expect. As a result of spending time with God and caring for your students enough to pray for them, you will be changed.

GOD'S Little Lessons for Teachers

Renewal

Cast away from you all the transgressions which you have committed against me, and get yourselves a new heart and a new spirit!

Ezekiel 18:31 RSV

Be made new in the attitude of your minds; and . . . put on the new self, created to be like God in true righteousness and holiness.

Ephesians 4:23-24

150

Brothers, I do not consider myself yet to have taken hold of it. But one thing I do: Forgetting what is behind and straining toward what is ahead, I press on toward the goal to win the prize for which God has called me heavenward in Christ Jesus.

Philippians 3:13-14

You have taken off your old self with its practices and have put on the new self, which is being renewed in knowledge in the image of its Creator.

Colossians 3:9-10

Grow in Grace

The story is told of a king who owned a valuable diamond—one of the rarest and most perfect in the world. One day the diamond fell, and a deep scratch marred its face. The king summoned the best diamond experts in the land to correct the blemish, but they all agreed they could not remove the scratch without cutting away a good part of the surface, thus reducing the weight and value of the diamond.

Finally one expert appeared and assured him that he could fix the diamond without reducing its value. His confidence was convincing, and the king gave the diamond to the man. In a few days, the artisan returned the diamond to the king, who was amazed to find that the ugly scratch was gone, and in its place a beautiful rose was etched. The former scratch had become the stem of an exquisite flower!

151

Any mistake you make in life may temporarily mar your reputation. But if you stick to what you know is right and continue to conform your will to God's, you can trust Him to turn the "scratches" on your soul into part of His signature—that's what it means to grow in God's grace.

GOD'S Little Lessons for Teachers

Restoration

Restore to me the joy of thy salvation, and uphold me with a willing spirit. . . . The sacrifice acceptable to God is a broken spirit; a broken and contrite heart, O God, thou wilt not despise.

Psalm 51:12,17 RSV

Our God, make us strong again! Smile on us and save us.

Psalm 80:3 CEV

152   Turn us back to You, O LORD, and we will be restored; Renew our days as of old.

Lamentations 5:21 NKJV

The God of all grace, who called you to his eternal glory in Christ, after you have suffered a little while, while himself restore you and make you strong, firm and steadfast.

1 Peter 5:10

The Great American Dream

om Chappell, founder of Tom's of Maine, was a man who seemed to have fulfilled "the great American dream." He had a wonderful family, a large New England home, and all the usual trappings of wealth. But he wasn't happy.

One day, Tom awoke and realized he had lost his enthusiasm. Not only that, he had started to question why he was in business. Tom embarked on a search for meaning for his life and work. He enrolled in divinity school, and one of the ideas he confronted was that making money did not have to be an empty, unfulfilling exercise. He developed a mission statement for his company that embraced social responsibility and care for the environment. In the process, Tom rediscovered his enthusiasm for his business and went on to introduce several new products that were well received. Work became more meaningful and more fun.

153

If you have lost enthusiasm for teaching, ask yourself why. Consider writing a mission statement for yourself. Recapture the important meaning of why you became a teacher.

GOD'S Little Lessons for Teachers

Restoration

He restores my soul.

Psalm 23:3 NKJV

Change your life. Turn to God and be baptized,
each of you, in the name of Jesus Christ, so
your sins are forgiven. Receive the gift of
the Holy Spirit.

Acts 2:38 THE MESSAGE

154

Cast away from you all your transgressions,
whereby ye have transgressed; and make you
a new heart and a new spirit.

Ezekiel 18:31 KJV

Turn to God! Give up your sins, and you will
be forgiven. Then that time will come when
the Lord will give you fresh strength.

Acts 3:19-20 CEV

Life-giving Words

Christian TV personality once participated in a two-week crusade in Boston. While standing at the back of the hall after the evening's meeting, a couple walked up to her. They looked at each other, and then the wife threw her arms around the woman and began to say, "Thank you, thank you, thank you."

The well-known woman was overwhelmed until the husband explained:

Two years ago, we were struggling financially. I had lost my job; it was a mess. I couldn't see a way out so I decided to make one. I decided to take my life. I checked into a cheap motel, and I had a gun. I was so desperate. I turned on the television and there you were. I hated Christian TV, but you said that God loved me. You told me that no matter how far away I felt, God loved me. I prayed with you, and I gave my life to God that night.

155

Before she knew it, the woman was in tears herself. Sharing the Word of God in front of the cameras rarely gave her insight into just how God was using His own Word in the lives of those beyond the cameras.

We never fully know just how, when, and to what end God uses our words as teachers, but we can be assured that He uses them mightily, especially when they are based on His Word, the Bible.[40]

GOD'S Little Lessons for Teachers

Self-discipline

Do not give in to bodily passions, which are
always at war against the soul.

1 Peter 2:11 TEV

Everything in the world—the cravings of sinful
man, the lust of his eyes and the boasting of
what he has and does—comes not from the
Father but from the world.

1 John 2:16

156   Let my heart be blameless regarding Your statutes,
That I may not be ashamed.

Psalm 119:80 NKJV

Those who belong to Christ Jesus have crucified
their own sinful selves. They have given up their
old selfish feelings and the evil things they
wanted to do.

Galatians 5:24 NCV

Give Yourself a Check-up

 young boy walked into a drugstore one day and asked to use the telephone. He dialed a number and said, "Hello, Dr. Anderson, do you want to hire a boy to cut your grass and run errands for you?" After a pause he said, "Oh, you already have a boy? Are you completely satisfied with the job he's doing?" Another pause. "All right then, good-bye, Doctor."

As the boy thanked the druggist and prepared to leave, the druggist called to him. "Just a minute, son. I couldn't help but overhear your conversation. If you are looking for work, I could use a boy like you."

157

"Thank you, sir," the boy replied, "but I already have a job."

"You do?" the druggist responded. "But didn't you just try to get a job from Dr. Anderson?"

"No, sir," the boy said. "I already work for Dr. Anderson. I was just checking up on myself."

Encourage your students to become self-disciplined individuals who look for ways to improve performance and avoid mistakes. Teach them to ask others to give them suggestions on how they might do better, achieve more, and grow to the next level. Remind them that when they check up on themselves, others won't feel it necessary to do so!

GOD'S Little Lessons for Teachers

Self-discipline

God did not give us a spirit of timidity, but a spirit of power, of love and of self-discipline.
2 Timothy 1:7

I advise you to obey only the Holy Spirit's instructions. He will tell you where to go and what to do, and then you won't always be doing the wrong things your evil nature wants you to.
Galatians 5:16 TLB

158   Control yourselves and be careful! The devil, your enemy, goes around like a roaring lion looking for someone to eat. Refuse to give in to him, by standing strong in your faith.
1 Peter 5:8-9 NCV

Let the Lord Jesus Christ take control of you, and don't think of ways to indulge your evil desires.
Romans 13:14 NLT

You Can Fly

Michael Stone had always dreamed of flying. A young man of extreme dedication and discipline, Michael chose to pursue the "flying" of pole vaulting. At age fourteen, he began a regimented program to achieve his goal. He worked out every other day with weights, and on alternate days, he ran. Michael's father, his coach and trainer, monitored the program. Besides being an athlete, Michael was also an honor-roll student, and he helped his parents with their farm.

At age seventeen, Michael faced his greatest athletic challenge. People watched as the pole was set at 17 feet—several inches higher than Michael's personal best. He cleared it, and then he cleared the pole at 17 feet 2 inches and again at 17 feet 4 inches.

159

In his final vault, Michael needed to fly 9 inches higher than he ever had before. Taking deep breaths to relax, he sprinted down the runway to an effortless takeoff. He began to fly and cleared the bar, setting a new National and International Junior Olympics record. His years of practice and self-discipline in pursuit of a goal had resulted in victory, one made even sweeter by the fact that Michael Stone is blind.

Encourage your students to choose to endure today in the pursuit of their goals. Help them develop the self-discipline they need to be a success.

GOD'S Little Lessons for Teachers

Self-pity

"Let not your heart be troubled; you believe in God, believe also in Me."

John 14:1 NKJV

God has made us what we are. In Christ Jesus, God made us to do good works, which God planned in advance for us to live our lives doing.

Ephesians 2:10 NCV

160

We are afflicted in every way, but not crushed; perplexed, but not despairing; persecuted, but not forsaken; struck down, but not destroyed.

2 Corinthians 4:8-9 NASB

We say with confidence, "The Lord is my helper; I will not be afraid. What can man do to me?"

Hebrews 13:6

ABCDEFGHIJKLMNOPQRSTUVWXYZ

Don't Despair

While in the midst of contending with the geographic problems of building the Panama Canal, Colonel George Washington Goethals had to endure a great deal of criticism from those back home who predicted he would never complete his great task. The visionary builder continued on, refusing to give in to their doomsday attitudes or to succumb to self-pity because of their carping.

"Aren't you going to answer your critics?" a reporter asked him.

"In time I will," Goethals replied.

"How? And when?" the reporter inquired.

161

The colonel merely smiled and said simply, "I'll answer my detractors with a finished canal."

In the same way Ole Bull, a violinist in the nineteenth century, was once offered space in the *New York Herald* to answer his critics. He said, "I think it is best that they write against me. I shall play against them."

If someone criticizes your work in the classroom, continue to do the very best you can do—consistently, persistently, and insistently. Diligent performance disarms criticism and debilitates self-pity. It wastes no time and suffers no loss. Make your steady, faithful work your best defense. It not only will prove your critics wrong, but also strengthen your resolve and build your self-esteem.

ABCDEFGHIJKLMNOPQRSTUVWXYZ

GOD'S Little Lessons for Teachers

Self-pity

Those who wait on the LORD Shall renew their strength; They shall mount up with wings like eagles, They shall run and not be weary, They shall walk and not faint.

Isaiah 40:31 NKJV

"Peace I leave with you, my peace I give unto you: not as the world giveth, give I unto you. Let not your heart be troubled, neither let it be afraid."

John 14:27 KJV

162

I will give them a crown to replace their ashes, and the oil of gladness to replace their sorrow, and clothes of praise to replace their spirit of sadness.

Isaiah 61:3 NCV

I have learned, in whatsoever state I am, therewith to be content.

Philippians 4:11 KJV

Different Outlook, Different Outcome

Kevin was a high school football star and later, an avid wrestler, boxer, hunter, and skin-diver. Then tragically, a broken neck left him paralyzed from the chest down. His doctors were hopeful that one day, he would be able to walk with the help of braces and crutches.

The former athlete could not reconcile himself to his physical limitations, however, so he prevailed upon two of his friends to leave him alone in a wooded area. After they left, he held a twelve-gauge shotgun to his abdomen and pulled the trigger, committing suicide at the age of twenty-four.

At the age of nineteen, Jim was stabbed, leaving him paralyzed from the middle of his chest down. Although confined to a wheelchair, he lives alone, cooks his own meals, washes his clothes, and cleans his house. He drives himself in a specially equipped automobile. He has written three books and was the photographer for the first book on the history of wheelchair sports. Thirty years after his injury, he made a successful parachute jump, landing precisely on his target.

163

Kevin and Jim had nearly identical injuries and physical limitations. Their outlook, however, led to vastly different outcomes.

What is your outlook on life today? A positive attitude will improve the overall atmosphere of your classroom, and because of your Godly example, your students will learn to look at the bright side of every challenging situation.

GOD'S Little Lessons for Teachers

Shame

Fear not; you will no longer live in shame.
The shame of your youth . . . will be
remembered no more.

Isaiah 54:4 TLB

No one whose hope is in you will ever be put
to shame, but they will be put to shame who
are treacherous without excuse.

Psalm 25:3

164

May those who hope in you not be disgraced
because of me, O LORD, the LORD Almighty;
may those who seek you not be put to shame.

Psalm 69:6

See, I lay in Zion a stone that causes men to
stumble and a rock that makes them fall, and the
one who trusts in him will never be put to shame.

Romans 9:33

Down in the Mire

D. L. Moody told the story of a Chinese convert who gave this testimony:

I was down in a deep pit crying for someone to help me out. As I looked up, I saw a gray-haired man looking down at me. I said, "Can you help me out?" "My son," he replied, "I am Confucius. If you had read my books and followed what I taught, you would never have fallen into this dreadful pit." Then he was gone.

Soon I saw another man coming. "My son," Buddha said, "forget about yourself. Get into a state of rest. Then, my child, you will be in a delicious state just as I am." "Yes," I said, "I will do that when I am above this mire. Can you help me out?" I looked, and he was gone.

165

I was beginning to sink into despair when I saw another figure above me. There were marks of suffering on His face. "My child," He said, "what is the matter?" But before I could reply, He was down in the mire by my side. He folded His arms about me and lifted. He did not say, "Shame on you for falling into that pit." Instead He said, "We will walk on together now."

If you are facing a problem in your classroom, turn it over to God; He will not let you be put to shame. Allow Him to move on your behalf, and watch Him give you the victory over the situation.

GOD'S Little Lessons for Teachers

Shame

Do your best to present yourself to God as one approved, a workman who does not need to be ashamed and who correctly handles the word of truth.

2 Timothy 2:15

Then, when that happens, we are able to hold our heads high no matter what happens and know that all is well, for we know how dearly God loves us, and we feel this warm love everywhere within us because God has given us the Holy Spirit to fill our hearts with his love.

Romans 5:5 TLB

166

THEREFORE being justified by faith, we have peace with God through our Lord Jesus Christ.

Romans 5:1 KJV

We have renounced secret and shameful ways; we do not use deception, nor do we distort the word of God. On the contrary, by setting forth the truth plainly we commend ourselves to every man's conscience in the sight of God.

2 Corinthians 4:2

The Parts of a Successful Life

Wallace E. Johnson, president of Holiday Inns and one of America's most successful builders, once said:

I always keep on a card in my billfold the following verses and refer to them frequently: "Ask, and it shall be given you; seek, and ye shall find; knock, and it shall be opened unto you: For every one that asketh receiveth; and he that seeketh findeth; and to him that knocketh it shall be opened" (Matthew 7:7-8 KJV).

These verses are among God's greatest promises. Yet they are a little one-sided. They indicate a philosophy of receiving, but not of giving. One day as my wife, Alma, and I were seeking God's guidance for a personal problem, I came across the following verse which has since been a daily reminder to me of what my responsibility as a businessman is to God: "Study to shew thyself approved unto God, a workman that needeth not to be ashamed, rightly dividing the word of truth" (2 Timothy 2:15 KJV).

167

Since then I have measured my actions against the phrase: "A workman that needeth not to be ashamed."

As a teacher, what standard do you measure your actions against?

GOD'S Little Lessons for Teachers

Speech

Let your speech always be gracious, seasoned with salt, so that you may know how you ought to answer every one.

Colossians 4:6 RSV

The mouth of the righteous man utters wisdom, and his tongue speaks what is just.

Psalm 37:30

168

Whoso keepeth his mouth and his tongue, keepeth his soul from troubles.

Proverbs 21:23 KJV

You must understand this, my beloved: let everyone be quick to listen, slow to speak, slow to anger.

James 1:19 NRSV

No Mayo

While preparing to speak at a convention, a woman wanted her husband to go out for sandwiches while she got ready for the event. She requested a chicken sandwich with no mayonnaise. She made sure he understood the order, even to the point of his replying, "Yep, I got it. N-o-o-o-o mayo."

When the sandwich arrived, however, she found it smothered with mayonnaise. She launched into a tirade of "you never listen—you only care about yourself" statements. Tension filled the air in their hotel room for a full hour before she finally asked her husband to forgive her.

169

Later that evening after she had spoken, a woman came to her and said, "It's lovely to see how much you and your husband love each other. Treasure one another!" She walked away with tears in her eyes.

A woman standing nearby said, "She lost her husband last month. They had been married only two years."

The speaker thought, *How would I feel if the last thing I got to say to my husband was that he blew my sandwich order?*

What was the last thing you said to your students as they walked out of the classroom? Express gratitude for their lives rather than irritation with their faults.[41]

GOD'S Little Lessons for Teachers

Speech

A soft answer turns away wrath, but a harsh word stirs up anger.

Proverbs 15:1 NRSV

But the tongue can no man tame; it is an unruly evil, full of deadly poison.

James 3:8 KJV

How great a forest is set abalze by a small fire! And the tongue is a fire!

James 3:5-6 NRSV

Let the words of my mouth, and the meditation of my heart, be acceptable in thy sight, O LORD, my strength, and my redeemer.

Psalm 19:14

Defensive Words

The horned lizard uses a distinctive defense mechanism against aggressors. First, the lizard hisses and swells its body with air. If that doesn't work, the animal flattens its body into a dorsal shield and tips it up toward the attacker, projecting an image that would be difficult to swallow. When all else fails, the lizard's eyelids suddenly swell shut. A hair-like stream of blood comes shooting out from an opening near the animal's eyelids and is aimed directly at the enemy. The blood contains compounds that repel the attacker. Then the eyelids shrink back to a normal size.

171

People are not so different. Those who feel themselves under attack often rise to their full height, jut out their jaws, clench their fists, and "square off" for a fight. Angry words then spew out, aimed at the greatest area of vulnerability in the other person's life.

Our words of criticism, ridicule, and name-calling may stop or stall an attack, but they never bring peace, reconciliation, or resolution. Only uplifting and positive words spoken with genuine love bring peace and harmony to a classroom or faculty lounge. Choose to speak healing words today.[42]

GOD'S Little Lessons for Teachers

Spiritual Growth

Let us stop going over the same old ground again and again, always teaching those first lessons about Christ. Let us go on instead to other things and become mature in our understanding, as strong Christians ought to be.

Hebrews 6:1 TLB

Practice these things and devote yourself to them, in order that your progress may be seen by all.

1 Timothy 4:15 TEV

172

Study to shew thyself approved unto God, a workman that needeth not to be ashamed, rightly dividing the word of truth.

2 Timothy 2:15 KJV

Open my eyes to see the wonderful truths in your law.

Psalm 119:18 NLT

Back-stage Homework

Several years ago, well-known author and pastor Bill Hybels played on a park district football team. He was assigned to play defensive middle linebacker, which was fine with him since his favorite professional athlete was Mike Singletary, all-pro middle linebacker for the Chicago Bears.

Hybels writes in *Honest to God:*

I crouched low and stared intently at the quarterback, readying myself to explode into the middle of the action in typical Singletary style. The battle raged . . . and reality struck with a vengeance. Using a simple head fake, the quarterback sent me in the opposite direction of the play, and the offense gained fifteen yards. So went the rest of the game. By the fourth quarter, I came to a brilliant conclusion: If I wanted to play football like Mike Singletary, I would have to do more than try to mimic his on-the-field actions. I would have to get behind the scenes, and practice like he practiced. I would have to lift weights and run laps like he did. I would have to memorize plays and study films as he did. If I wanted his success on the field, I would have to pursue his disciplines off the field.

No teacher can be a classroom "star" without back-stage homework. The same is true in the Christian life.[43]

173

GOD'S Little Lessons for Teachers

Spiritual Growth

Put on all of God's armor so that you will be able to stand firm against all strategies and tricks of the Devil.

Ephesians 6:11 NLT

Grow in grace, and in the knowledge of our Lord and Savior Jesus Christ. To him be glory both now and for ever. Amen.

2 Peter 3:18 KJV

174   The righteous man will flourish like the palm tree, He will grow like a cedar in Lebanon.

Psalm 92:12 NASB

This is my prayer: that your love may abound more and more in knowledge and depth of insight, so that you may be able to discern what is best and may be pure and blameless until the day of Christ.

Philippians 1:9-10

Deep Roots

any people see abundant spring rains as a great blessing to farmers, especially if the rains come after the plants have sprouted and are several inches tall. What they don't realize is that even a short drought can have a devastating effect on a crop of seedlings that has received too much rain.

Why? Because during frequent rains, the young plants are not required to push their roots deeper into the soil in search of water. If a drought occurs later, plants with shallow root systems will quickly die.

175

We often receive abundance in our lives—rich fellowship, great teaching, thorough "soakings" of spiritual blessings. Yet when stress or tragedy enters our lives, we may find ourselves thinking God has abandoned us or is unfaithful. The fact is, we have allowed the "easiness" of our lives to keep us from pushing our spiritual roots deeper. We have allowed others to spoon-feed us, rather than develop our own deep personal relationship with God through prayer and study of His Word.

Only the deeply rooted are able to endure hard times without wilting. The best advice is to enjoy the "rain" while seeking to grow even closer to God.

GOD'S Little Lessons for Teachers

Stability

He will not fear evil tidings; His heart is steadfast, trusting in the LORD.

Psalm 112:7 NASB

Grass withers and flowers fade, but the word of our God endures forever.

Isaiah 40:8 TEV

He who doubts is like a wave of the sea, blown and tossed by the wind. . . . he is a double-minded man, unstable in all he does.

176

James 1:6,8

When there is moral rot within a nation, its government topples easily; but with honest, sensible leaders there is stability.

Proverbs 28:2 TLB

A Promise Kept

Stephen Covey once counseled a man who had a reputation for procrastination and selfishness. The man could rarely be counted on to keep his commitments. Covey challenged him to a simple change. "Will you get up in the morning when you say you're planning to get up?" Covey asked. "Will you just get up in the morning?"

The man saw little point in what Covey was challenging him to do, but when Covey asked him to commit to getting up at a certain time for a week, the man agreed to do so.

177

Covey saw the man a week later and asked, "Did you do it?" The man replied in the affirmative, so Covey then asked, "What's the next thing you're going to commit to do?"

Little by little, the man began to make and keep commitments. No one knew of the plan but Covey and one friend. Over time, the man made remarkable changes. His relationships improved, his promises were kept, and his integrity was regained. His entire life stabilized because he began to keep his promises—first to himself and then to others.

When you keep your word to yourself, it becomes easier to keep your word to your students, and it produces tremendous peace of mind and stability in your life and your classroom.

GOD'S Little Lessons for Teachers

Stability

By justice a king gives a country stability, but one who is greedy for bribes tears it down.

Proverbs 29:4

Wisdom and knowledge will be the stability of your times, And the strength of salvation; The fear of the LORD *is* His treasure.

Isaiah 33:6 NKJV

178

"The eye is a light for the body. If your eyes are good, your whole body will be full of light. But if your eyes are evil, your whole body will be full of darkness."

Matthew 6:22-23 NCV

Be steadfast, immovable, always abounding in the work of the Lord, knowing that your labor is not in vain in the Lord.

1 Corinthians 15:58 NKJV

Small Bits Matter a Lot

Have you ever watched an icicle form on a cold winter day? Did you notice how the dripping water froze, one drop at a time, until the icicle was a foot long, or more? If the water was clean, the icicle remained clear and sparkled brightly in the sun; but if the water was slightly muddy, the icicle looked cloudy, its beauty spoiled.

In just this manner our character is formed. Each thought or feeling adds its influence. Each decision we make, whether about matters great or small, will contribute to our singular identity. The things that we take into our minds and souls—be they impressions, experiences, visual images, or the words of others—will all help to create our character.

179

As teachers, we must remain concerned at all times about the "droplets" that influence our students. In large part these small bits of experience shape the stability or instability of their lives. Help them to realize that habits of hate, falsehood, and evil intent will mar them like the muddied icicle, eventually destroying them. Encourage them to develop habits of love, truth, and goodness that will silently mold and fashion them into the image of God and give them a firm foundation, building their characters like the crystal-clear icicle.

GOD'S Little Lessons for Teachers

Strength

The LORD is my rock, and my fortress, and my deliverer; my God, my strength, in whom I will trust; my buckler, and the horn of my salvation, and my high tower.

Psalm 18:2 KJV

He gives strength to those who are tired and more power to those who are weak.

Isaiah 40:29 NCV

180   My soul melts from heaviness; Strengthen me according to Your word.

Psalm 119:28 NKJV

I have the strength to face all conditions by the power that Christ gives me.

Philippians 4:13 TEV

Teamwork

CBS newsman Charles Osgood once told a story of two women who lived in the same convalescent center. Each had suffered a debilitating stroke. Ruth's stroke damaged her right side; Margaret's stroke restricted her left side.

Both Ruth and Margaret had once been accomplished pianists, but their strokes had forced them to face the fact that they might never play again. Then the convalescent center director asked the two women to try playing the center's piano together, Ruth taking the left-hand part and Margaret the right. They did, and the music they made together was beautiful. A friendship developed, and both women felt a renewal of meaning and joy in their lives.

181

As Christians, we are called to work together with other believers—sharing our strengths with others and in turn receiving strength from them in our areas of weakness. In this way, the entire Body of Christ is made strong and effective, and the specific needs of each individual are met. Oftentimes, you can accomplish the difficult or seemingly impossible tasks in your school if you will utilize the talents and strengths of other teachers.[44]

GOD'S Little Lessons for Teachers

Strength

My flesh and my heart may fail, but God is the strength of my heart and my portion forever.

Psalm 73:26

You armed me with strength for battle; you made my adversaries bow at my feet.

2 Samuel 22:40

It is God that girdeth me with strength, and maketh my way perfect.

182

Psalm 18:32 KJV

[Jesus said]: "My grace is sufficient for you, for my power is made perfect in weakness." Therefore I will boast all the more gladly about my weaknesses, so that Christ's power may rest on me.

2 Corinthians 12:9

Amazing Strength

young man was running a race, and he found himself falling farther and farther behind his competitors. His friends cheered him on from the sidelines, but to no avail. Then suddenly, his lips began to move, his legs picked up speed, and to the amazement of the entire crowd watching the race, he passed his competitors one by one—and won the race!

After he had been awarded a blue ribbon and received the congratulations of his coach and teammates, he turned to his friends. One of them asked, "We could see your lips moving, but we couldn't make out what you were saying. What were you mumbling out there?"

183

The young man replied, "Oh, I was talking to God. I told Him, 'Lord, You pick 'em up, and I'll put 'em down. . . . You pick 'em up, and I'll put 'em down!"

When you live your life the way you know God's Word commands you, and when you are believing to the best of your ability that the Lord will help you be an effective teacher, you are then in a position to know with certainty what the Apostle Paul knew: "I can do all things through Christ which strengtheneth me" (Philippians 4:13 KJV).

GOD'S Little Lessons for Teachers

Stress

In my distress I cried out to the LORD. . . .
He heard me from his sanctuary; my cry
reached his ears.

2 Samuel 22:7 NLT

Jesus said, "Don't let your hearts be troubled.
Trust in God, and trust in me."

John 14:1 NCV

184

Leave your troubles with the LORD, and he
will defend you; he never lets honest people
be defeated.

Psalm 55:22 TEV

Fear not, for I am with you. Do not be dismayed.
I am your God. I will strengthen you; I will
help you; I will uphold you with my victorious
right hand.

Isaiah 41:10 TLB

Maintaining Control

Chuck Givens was on his way to conduct a workshop some two hundred miles from his home. He left in plenty of time and looked forward to the drive. He enjoyed taking the tight mountain curves in his sports car. On that particular day, however, his fan belt broke, and the car immediately overheated. Nevertheless, he decided to press on in hopes of finding a gas station with a fan belt.

A few minutes later, the engine froze. He faced another choice. He could call and cancel his workshop, or he could try to get to his destination some other way. He decided to hitchhike. Although there wasn't much traffic, within ten minutes a car stopped. Not only did the driver deliver him to his exact destination, but the driver decided to enroll in the workshop!

185

At the end of the program, he asked those in attendance, "Is anybody heading my way?" Ten hands shot up. He got a ride home. At the day's close, he felt calm and successful, rather than angry and frustrated.

This lesson is especially pertinent for teachers. Events control our classrooms only if we give them that power. It's often better to face the challenge of pressing on, rather than to become buried in the problem of the moment.[45]

GOD'S Little Lessons for Teachers

Stress

In the day of my trouble I will call upon You,
For You will answer me.

Psalm 86:7 NKJV

Let us not become weary in doing good, for at
the proper time we will reap a harvest if we do
not give up.

Galatians 6:9

186

Consider it all joy, my brethren, when you
encounter various trials, knowing that the
testing of your faith produces endurance.

James 1:2-3 NASB

"Come to me, all of you who are weary and
carry heavy burdens, and I will give you rest."

Matthew 11:28 NLT

Seeking Serenity

n 1975, an American doctor was invited to attend a conference in Finland. The conference was aimed at better understanding why heart disease was at epidemic proportions in Finland. At a banquet held during the conference, Finland's president asked the doctor if he could explain the reason for this disturbing trend.

"Finland," the doctor said, "has gone to war thirty-nine times in two hundred years. And Finland has never won!" The doctor went on to cite the fact that the Finns bordered the Soviet Union at that time. In fact, the closer a Finn lived to the border, the more likely he or she was to die prematurely. In 1944, the Soviets had annexed a fifty-mile-wide strip of Finland, property that was a beloved home to many Finns. The people who were forcibly relocated never adjusted to this loss in their hearts and minds. Stress was a constant in their lives, and the stress, in turn, was linked to heart problems.

187

Don't allow students to dictate your mood—or your stress level. Instead pray, *God grant me the serenity to accept the things I cannot change, the courage to change the things I can, and the wisdom to know the difference.*[46]

GOD'S Little Lessons for Teachers

Success

It is very good if a man has received wealth from the Lord, and the good health to enjoy it. To enjoy your work and to accept your lot in life—that is indeed a gift from God.

Ecclesiastes 5:19 TLB

Riches and honor are with me, enduring wealth and prosperity. My fruit is better than gold, even fine gold, and my yield than choice silver.

Proverbs 8:18-19 RSV

188

The mind of man plans his way, But the LORD directs his steps.

Proverbs 16:9 NASB

Wealth and riches are in his house, and his righteousness endures forever.

Psalm 112:3

Truly Satisfying?

n a *Peanuts* comic strip by Charles Shultz, Charlie Brown tells Lucy about his birdhouse project, saying, "Well, I'm a lousy carpenter. I can't nail straight. I can't saw straight, and I always split the wood. I'm nervous, I lack confidence, I'm stupid, I have poor taste, and absolutely no sense of design."

Then in the last frame of the strip he concludes, "So, all things considered, it's coming along okay."

Although we may not go to this extreme, many people take this same approach to life and work. They view their job as merely a step toward being able to do what they really want to do—enduring the Monday-to-Friday grind in order to "live" on the weekend. This attitude of "making a living" rather than making every moment of your life count for something results in a general sense of unfulfillment in life itself.

189

Choose work that is truly satisfying. If teaching isn't something you really enjoy and find fulfilling, choose a career that is rewarding for you, not only financially, but mentally, emotionally, and spiritually. Life is too short to waste effort on the *majority* of your days solely to enjoy the *minority* of your days. Live each day with maximum effort, diligence, and performance.[47]

GOD'S Little Lessons for Teachers

Success

"I know the plans I have for you," declares the
LORD, "plans to prosper you and not to harm
you, plans to give you hope and a future."

Jeremiah 29:11

True humility and respect for the Lord lead a
man to riches, honor and long life.

Proverbs 22:4 TLB

190   They are like trees growing beside a stream, trees
that produce fruit in season and always have leaves.
Those people succeed in everything they do.

Psalm 1:3 CEV

The Lord your God will make you most prosperous
in all the work of your hands and in the fruit of
your womb, the young of your livestock and the
crops of your land.

Deuteronomy 30:9

Faith in People

n the campaign of 1948, nobody in either political party—not a professional politician, not a reporter, not even his own mother-in-law—doubted that Tom Dewey would be the next president of the United States. A *Newsweek* poll of political commentators predicted the final vote: Dewey, 50, Truman, 0.

No president in office had ever campaigned so hard or traveled as many miles as Truman, who was sixty-four years old. Younger men on the train with candidate Truman described it as the worst ordeal of their lives. The roadbed was rough, and Truman insisted the train fly at eighty miles an hour during the night to reach as many destinations as possible. The food was bad, and the work was unrelenting. The only reason any of the staff stuck by Truman was Truman himself. There was something about his heroic, memorable act of faith in the American public that compelled them to stick with him. As he crisscrossed the nation, Truman reminded his fellow countrymen, "Here I am, here's what I stand for. Here's what I'm going to do if you keep me in the job. You decide." Despite the odds against him, Truman won the election.

No success in life, including academic and career success, is ever maintained without an effort equal to that required to attain it.[48]

191

GOD'S Little Lessons for Teachers

Temptation

Be self-controlled and alert. Your enemy the devil prowls around like a roaring lion looking for someone to devour. Resist him, standing firm in the faith, because you know that your brothers throughout the world are undergoing the same kind of sufferings.

1 Peter 5:8-9

The Lord knows how to rescue godly men from trials and to hold the unrighteous for the day of judgment, while continuing their punishment.

2 Peter 2:9

192

"Watch and pray so that you will not fall into temptation. The spirit is willing, but the body is weak."

Mark 14:38

Submit yourselves therefore to God. Resist the devil and he will flee from you.

James 4:7 RSV

ABCDEFGHIJKLMNOPQRSTUVWXYZ

Tempting Choices, Right Decisions

As college roommates, Meg and Ann became best friends. Then one day, Meg told her that John had asked her for a date. Ann was disappointed because she'd had a crush on him for two years. Still, she managed to say, "Have a good time," and later, she put on a happy face at their wedding.

Through the years, the girls remained close. Ann enjoyed teasing and laughing with John, so when Meg asked her to join them at a beachside bungalow for a week, she jumped at the chance. One afternoon when Meg went out to visit a friend, Ann and John betrayed her trust. Afterward, Ann felt sick inside.

193

A few minutes of flirtation and passion resulted in more than a decade of misery for Ann. She might never have known happiness again if Meg hadn't confronted her about her refusal to accept a marriage proposal. Ann sobbed, "I'm horrible. You don't know how I've wronged you."

Meg said, "I do know, Ann," and one look into her eyes confirmed that she had known, had loved, and had forgiven.

Temptation itself is not a sin, but allowing it to continue is. God always provides a way of escape; you must simply take it.

ABCDEFGHIJKLMNOPQRSTUVWXYZ

GOD'S Little Lessons for Teachers

Temptation

No temptation has overtaken you that is not common to man. God is faithful, and he will not let you be tempted beyond your strength, but with the temptation will also provide the way of escape, that you may be able to endure it.

1 Corinthians 10:13 RSV

Since he himself has now been through suffering and temptation, he knows what it is like when we suffer and are tempted, and he is wonderfully able to help us.

Hebrews 2:18 TLB

194

"Lead us not into temptation, but deliver us from evil: For thine is the kingdom, and the power, and the glory, for ever. Amen."

Matthew 6:13 KJV

Consider him who endured such opposition from sinful men, so that you will not grow weary and lose heart. In your struggle against sin, you have not yet resisted to the point of shedding your blood.

Hebrews 12:3-4

Stay Out of the Pig Pen

Farmers have a saying that goes something like, "Once you're standing in the pig pen, it's a little too late to worry about soiling your Sunday clothes." And that sound piece of advice carries beyond the farm. The key to avoiding wrong doing and compromise is to decide in advance to stay as far away from it as possible.

Impropriety has a way of revealing itself a little at a time. Once we get to thinking that some form of wrong doing is "not so bad," it's often just a few more steps to the pig pen, with little hope of escaping without getting dirty.

195

Teach your students to resist even the appearance of wrong doing whenever they encounter it and to decide ahead of time how they would handle hypothetical situations. Would they cheat on a test? Would they lie to their parents? Instruct them not to listen to people who say, "Everybody's doing it." Everybody isn't!

Teach your students that everyone encounters temptation. It's a fact of life. But they can successfully overcome temptation by identifying the "pig pens" they must face each day and by determining to stay as far away from them as possible. Remind them that an ounce of prevention can be worth ten pounds of purity.

GOD'S Little Lessons for Teachers

Thankfulness

Let your roots grow down into him and draw up nourishment from him. See that you go on growing in the Lord, and become strong and vigorous in the truth you were taught. Let your lives overflow with joy and thanksgiving for all he has done.

Colossians 2:7 TLB

Whatever you do or say, let it be as a representative of the Lord Jesus, and come with him into the presence of God the Father to give him your thanks.

Colossians 3:17 TLB

196

Thanks be to God, who gives us the victory through our Lord Jesus Christ.

1 Corinthians 15:57 NASB

The LORD is my strength and my shield; my heart trusts in him, and I am helped. My heart leaps for joy and I will give thanks to him in song.

Psalm 28:7

An Attitude of Gratitude

ulton Oursler told a story of an old nurse who was born a slave on the eastern shore of Maryland. She had not only attended Fulton's birth, but also that of his mother. He credits her for teaching him the greatest lesson he ever learned about thankfulness and contentment. Recalls Oursler:

I remember her as she sat at the kitchen table in our house—the hard, old, brown hands folded across her starched apron; the glistening eyes; and the husky old whispering voice, saying, "Much obliged, Lord, for my vittles."

"Anna," I asked, "what's a vittle?"

"It's what I've got to eat and drink—that's vittles," the old nurse replied.

"But you'd get your vittles whether you thanked the Lord or not."

"Sure," said Anna, "but it makes everything taste better to be thankful."

197

For many people, poverty is not a condition of the pocketbook, but a state of mind. Do you think of yourself as being rich or poor today? What do you value and count as "wealth" in your life? Impress upon your students that if they are thankful for what they have, then they are very wealthy indeed!

GOD'S Little Lessons for Teachers

Thankfulness

In everything give thanks; for this is the will of
God in Christ Jesus for you.

1 Thessalonians 5:18 NKJV

Give thanks to the LORD, for he is good; his love
endures forever.

Psalm 107:1

198

You have turned my mourning into joyful dancing.
You have taken away my clothes of mourning and
clothed me with joy, that I might sing praises to
you and not be silent. O LORD my God, I will
give you thanks forever!

Psalms 30:11-12 NLT

O come, let us sing for joy to the LORD; Let us
shout joyfully to the rock of our salvation. Let us
come before His presence with thanksgiving.

Psalms 95: 1-2 NASB

Radiating Sunshine

Early one morning in the locker room, Ruth overheard a cheerful voice say, "I really appreciate the book you picked up for me last week. I'm glad you suggested it." Then the voice went on to greet another person, "Good morning! Have you ever seen such a gorgeous day? I spied a pair of meadowlarks this morning."

Ruth imagined that only a wealthy woman with little to do could be that cheerful. As she rounded the corner, she came face to face with a woman in a yellow housekeeping uniform—the cleaning lady— who put in long hard days with mops, brooms, and buckets. Yet she radiated sunshine!

199

After her laps in the pool, Ruth sank down into the warm, foamy whirlpool. Her two companions were deep in conversation—one intent on describing his woes with arthritic knees, a heart problem, sleepless nights, and pain-filled days. The water was too hot for him, he complained, and the whirlpool jets weren't strong enough. His heavy diamond ring flashed in the light as he wiped his face with a monogrammed towel. Ruth made a comparison to the cleaning woman and wondered why the man was such a complainer when he had so much for which to be thankful.

Today, remember your blessings, and light up your classroom with a smile![49]

GOD'S Little Lessons for Teachers

Truth

Surely you heard of him and were taught in him in accordance with the truth that is in Jesus.
Ephesians 4:21

All Scripture is inspired by God and is useful for teaching the truth, rebuking error, correcting faults, and giving instruction for right living.
2 Timothy 3:16 TEV

200

The words of the LORD are flawless, like silver refined in a furnace of clay, purified seven times.
Psalm 12:6

The LORD hates . . . A proud look, A lying tongue, Hands that shed innocent blood.
Proverbs 6:16-17 NKJV

Making the Masters

n 1994, while competing in the Western Open, professional golfer Davis Love III moved his marker on a green to get it out of another player's putting line. A couple of holes later, he couldn't remember if he had moved his ball back to its original spot. Unsure, Love gave himself a one-stroke penalty.

That one stroke caused Love to miss the cut and be knocked out of the tournament. If he had made the cut and then finished last in the competition, he would have earned $2,000 that week. That amount came into play at the year's end. Love was $500 short in the annual winnings necessary to qualify for the following year's Master's Tournament. Love began 1995 needing to win a tournament in order to qualify for the event.

Someone asked Love how he would feel if he missed the Masters for calling a penalty on himself. Love said, "How would I feel if I won the Masters and wondered for the rest of my life if I cheated to get in?" As it turned out, the week before the 1995 Masters, Love won a tournament in New Orleans. Then in the Masters, he won $237,600 for finishing second.

Most teachers know the right thing to do. Be among the ones who actually have the courage to do it.[50]

201

GOD'S Little Lessons for Teachers

Truth

Do not testify falsely against your neighbor.

Exodus 20:16 NLT

Now, O Lord God, Thou art God, and Thy words are truth.

2 Samuel 7:28 NASB

We will lovingly follow the truth at all times—speaking truly, dealing truly, living truly—and so become more and more in every way like Christ.

Ephesians 4:15-16 TLB

202

Jesus answered,"I am the way and the truth and the life. No one comes to the Father except through me."

John 14:6

Such a Good Feeling

uthor Alice Walker once accidentally broke a fruit jar. Though there were several siblings around who could have done it, Alice's father turned to her and asked, "Did you break the jar, Alice?"

Alice said, "Looking into his large brown eyes, I knew that he wanted me to tell the truth. I also knew he might punish me if I did. But the truth inside of me wanted badly to be expressed. So I confessed."

Her father realized that the broken jar was an accident, so no punishment was administered. Yet what impressed Alice was the love she saw in her father's eyes when he knew that Alice had told the truth. "The love in his eyes rewarded and embraced me," Alice recalled. "Suddenly I felt an inner peace that I still recall with gratitude to this day whenever I am called upon to tell the truth."

203

A person always feels good after telling the truth, doing the noble thing, showing kindness, or meeting a need. You must remind your students, however, that they are to do what is right because it is right, not because it will make them feel better or bring them a reward—and that, is the truth.

GOD'S Little Lessons for Teachers

Wisdom

To be wise, you must have reverence for the Lord.
Job 28:28 TEV

If any of you needs wisdom, you should ask God
for it. He is generous and enjoys giving to all
people, so he will give you wisdom.
James 1:5 NCV

I will instruct you and teach you in the way you
should go; I will counsel you and watch over you.
Psalm 32:8

204

Determination to be wise is the first step toward
becoming wise! And with your wisdom, develop
common sense and good judgment.
Proverbs 4:7 TLB

Too Heavy

n *The Hiding Place,* Corrie ten Boom tells about a lesson she learned from her father one day while they were riding a train. She asked her father, "What is sex sin?"

Her father looked at her for a moment, then stood up, lifted his traveling case from the rack over their heads, and set it on the floor of the train car. "Will you carry it off the train, Corrie?" he asked.

Corrie stood up and began to tug at the case, which was filled with watches and spare parts he had purchased that morning. "It's too heavy," she said.

205

"Yes," he said, "and it would be a pretty poor father who would ask his little girl to carry such a load. It's the same way, Corrie, with knowledge. Some knowledge is too heavy for children. When you are older and stronger, you can bear it. For now you must trust me to carry it for you."

There are many issues and questions that children are too young to carry. Wisdom is knowing what knowledge is necessary and when and how it should be learned and applied. A good teacher is wise not to teach everything he or she knows and not to bother learning what is unimportant to teach.[51]

GOD'S Little Lessons for Teachers

Wisdom

I guide you in the way of wisdom and lead you along straight paths. When you walk, your steps will not be hampered; when you run, you will not stumble.

Proverbs 4:11-12

The Lord grants wisdom! His every word is a treasure of knowledge and understanding.

Proverbs 2:6 TLB

206

Your commands make me wiser than my enemies, because they are mine forever. I am wiser than all my teachers, because I think about your rules.

Psalms 119:98-99 NCV

What seems to be God's foolishness is wiser than human wisdom, and what seems to be God's weakness is stronger than human strength.

1 Corinthians 1:25 TEV

Doing What Is Best

At age sixty, Mary's mother developed severe pelvic pain. Exploratory surgery revealed osteoporosis, and Mary was told her mother would spend the rest of her life in a wheelchair.

Mary began to take over the chores of cleaning and cooking for her parents. One day her mother said to her, "Mary, unless you are just coming for a cup of tea and a chat, stop coming over here. I want you to stop cleaning my house, bringing me flowers, and cooking."

Mary asked, "Why don't you want me to help you? It's one way I can give back to you."

207

Her mother replied, "I want to let go of everything that looks like a reward for being sick. I want to heal. I'm going to put all of my energy into getting well and strong." Within six months, the doctors were amazed that her mother's pelvic bone was regenerating itself. A few months later, she was walking again. At age seventy-five, Mary's mother went sky-diving!

Mary learned that doing all she could to please her mother was not actually what was best for her mother. Before giving a student all the answers, we should ask God what He desires for that student and then line up our teaching efforts accordingly. Sometimes less immediate help yields long-term benefits.[52]

Work

Work hard and cheerfully at all you do, just as though you were working for the Lord and not merely for your masters, remembering that it is the Lord Christ who is going to pay you, giving you your full portion of all he owns. He is the one you are really working for.

Colossians 3:23-24 TLB

When God gives any man wealth and possessions, and enables him to enjoy them, to accept his lot and be happy in his work—this is a gift of God.

Ecclesiastes 5:19

208

"Don't work for food that spoils. Work for food that gives eternal life. The Son of Man will give you this food, because God the Father has given him the right to do so."

John 6:27 CEV

God is not unfair. He will not forget how hard you have worked for him and how you have shown your love to him by caring for other Christians, as you still do.

Hebrews 6:10 NLT

Encourage Willingness

 man once walked into a store and took his place in line behind four other customers. Before long, he realized the line wasn't moving. A trio of clerks behind the counter were involved in a personal discussion, and it was only after they sensed the restlessness of those waiting that they turned to give them attention. Even then, they did not offer service cheerfully. They acted as if the customers were interfering with their social lives and continued their personal conversation.

After making his purchase, the man asked to see the manager. Suddenly, the clerk's attitude changed. He became all smiles as he said, "I'm sorry if I kept you waiting."

209

The man smiled back and said, "Don't worry. It won't happen again. I can assure you it won't." If that sounded like a threat—it was. Little did the clerk know that he had neglected the owner of the store!

Most managers and teachers have tolerance for work that is not perfect, but few have tolerance for those who fail to show good effort or enthusiasm at their assigned tasks. A willing worker can be trained, even without the necessary experience. Encourage willingness in your students.[53]

GOD'S Little Lessons for Teachers

Work

Six days shall work be done: but the seventh day is the sabbath of rest, and holy convocation; ye shall do no work therein: it is the sabbath of the LORD in all your dwellings.

Leviticus 23:3 KJV

Each man's work will become evident; for the day will show it, because it is to be revealed with fire; and the fire itself will test the quality of each man's work.

210

I Corinthians 3:13 NASB

God has promised us a Sabbath when we will rest, even though it has not yet come. On that day God's people will rest from their work, just as God rested from his work.

Hebrews 4:9-10 CEV

Even when we were with you, we gave you this rule: "If a man will not work, he shall not eat."

2 Thessalonians 3:10

Making Time for Life

ost of us try to prove ourselves by working extra hard to get ahead. Yet despite our best efforts, the volume of work seems to increase geometrically. Not only do we find we're not moving ahead, but we often seem to not even be keeping pace! Rather than stop and regroup, oftentimes we push ahead and eventually burnout.

That's what happened to Denise. Her job ate up her life to the point where every surface in her home was cluttered with unfinished work. Each time a friend called, Denise had to cut the call short, claiming she had "too much work to do."

211

Finally, Denise's friends decided enough was enough. They showed up at her door one Saturday morning and announced, "We're the cleaning crew you've been meaning to call. We're going to help you get your life back." True to their word, they brought order back into Denise's life and even concluded the day with dinner at a fine restaurant. Their fee? A promise from Denise that she would stop neglecting her friends and make time for a "real" life.

Today, step back, regroup, clean off your teacher's desk, and reprioritize your life.[54]

GOD'S Little Lessons for Teachers

Worry

Don't worry about anything; instead, pray about everything; tell God your needs and don't forget to thank him for his answers.

Philippians 4:6 TLB

"Do not worry about tomorrow; it will have enough worries of its own. There is no need to add to the troubles each day brings."

Matthew 6:34 TEV

212

Give all your worries and cares to God, for he cares about what happens to you.

1 Peter 5:7 NLT

You will keep him in perfect peace, Whose mind is stayed on You, Because he trusts in You.

Isaiah 26:3 NKJV

Be Careful, Dad

 woman once recalled a number of admonitions she had heard down through the years from her father:

- Don't walk with a spoon in your mouth. You'll trip, and that spoon will go right down your throat.
- Don't race around that coffee table. You'll split your head on the corners. They should pad corners!
- Don't eat raw cookie dough. You might get salmonella poisoning.
- Did you wash your hands?
- Watch out for waiters. You don't want to get hot coffee poured on your head.
- Be sure to check the lead content of those mini-blinds you are buying.
- Watch how you use that cleaning fluid. It's poisonous.
- Watch your step when you board the train. You don't want to fall onto the tracks.

213

She has now realized that when her elderly father comes to visit and she takes him to the station to return home, she finds herself saying as she waves good-bye, "Be careful, Dad."

Concern for students and fellow teachers is a sign of love, but worry is a sign of doubt and fear. We each must learn the difference.[55]

GOD'S Little Lessons for Teachers

Worry

"The ones on whom seed was sown among the thorns; these are the ones who have heard the word, and the worries of the world, and the deceitfulness of riches, and the desires for other things enter in and choke the word, and it becomes unfruitful."

Mark 4:18-19 NASB

"You cannot add any time to your life by worrying about it."

Matthew 6:27 NCV

214

Have I not commanded you? Be strong and courageous! Do not tremble or be dismayed, for the LORD your God is with you wherever you go.

Joshua 1:9 NASB

"Peace I leave with you; my peace I give you. I do not give to you as the world gives. Do not let your hearts be troubled and do not be afraid."

John 14:27

No Turning Around

 young farmer was learning to plow. Seated on the tractor, he pulled the lever that dropped the plow to the ground and started across the field. After he had gone a few yards, he turned around to look at the furrow he was making. He was entranced by the rushing flow of rich black topsoil along the blade.

Too late, he caught himself and quickly turned back to look where he was going. He realized that in turning around to look at his work, he had strayed from his initial straight line. He pulled the tractor back into line, and then after a few more yards, he looked back at his furrow again. He repeated this process several times. By the time he reached the end of the field and turned the tractor around, he found he had created a wavering line that was of little use in plowing the rest of the field.

215

The young farmer soon learned that the only way to plow a straight furrow was to place his sights on a permanent marker across the field and keep the nose of his tractor squarely aimed at that point—no turning around to check his work!

We are wise when we set our sights on what God tells us to do and then do it with all of our might, leaving all the consequences of our teaching to Him.[56]

GOD'S Little Lessons for Teachers

Worship

Therefore, I urge you, brothers, in view of
God's mercy, to offer your bodies as living
sacrifices, holy and pleasing to God—this is
your spiritual act of worship.

Romans 12:1

God bought you with a high price. So you must
honor God with your body.

1 Corinthians 6:20 NLT

216   Spread for me a banquet of praise, serve High
God a feast of kept promises.

Psalm 50:15 THE MESSAGE

I will praise you, O Lord my God, with all my
heart; I will glorify your name forever.

Psalm 86:12

Autumn Dance

n *Mothering by Heart,* Robin Jones Gunn writes of this example of unashamed worship of our Creator:

She stood a short distance from her guardian at the park this afternoon, her distinctive features revealing that although her body blossomed into young adulthood, her mind would always remain a child's. My children ran and jumped and sifted sand through perfect, coordinated fingers. Caught up in fighting over a shovel, they didn't notice when the wind changed. But she did. A wild autumn wind spinning leaves into amber flurries.

I called to my boisterous son and jostled my daughter. Time to go. . . . My rosy-cheeked boy stood tall, watching with wide-eyed fascination the gyrating dance of the Down's syndrome girl as she scooped up leaves and showered herself with a twirling rain of autumn jubilation.

217

With each twist and hop she sang deep, earthy grunts—a canticle of praise meant only for the One whose breath causes the leaves to tremble from the trees.

Hurry up. Let's go. Seat belts on? I start the car. In the rearview mirror I study her one more time through misty eyes. And then the tears come. Not tears of pity for her. The tears are for me. For I am far too sophisticated to publicly shout praises to my Creator.

Take time each day to truly worship Him and to praise Him for His unique creations—your students!

GOD'S Little Lessons for Teachers

Worship

"Let your good deeds shine out for all to see, so that everyone will praise your heavenly Father."
Matthew 5:16 NLT

Whatever you do, work at it with all your heart, as working for the Lord, not for men.
Colossians 3:23

Come, let us bow down in worship, let us kneel before the LORD our Maker.
Psalm 95:6

218

Shout Hallelujah, you God-worshipers; give glory, you sons of Jacob; adore him, you daughters of Israel. He has never let you down, never looked the other way when you were being kicked around.
Psalms 22:23-24 THE MESSAGE

Worship and Worry

uth Bell Graham tells the story of when God taught her that worship is the antidote for worry. She was in a foreign country, wide-awake at 3 A.M., so she began to pray for one who was running away from God. She says, "When it is dark and the imagination runs wild, there are fears only a mother can understand."

Then suddenly, the Lord told her to "quit studying the problem and start studying the promises." So she opened her Bible and began to read Philippians 4:6 KJV: "Be careful for nothing; but in everything by prayer and supplication *with thanksgiving. . . .*" She recalls:

> Suddenly I realized the missing ingredient in my prayers had been "with thanksgiving." So I put down my Bible and spent time worshipping Him for Who and What He is. This covers more territory than any one mortal can comprehend. Even contemplating what little we do know dissolves doubts, reinforces faith, and restores joy. It was as if someone turned on the lights in my mind and heart, and the little fears and worries that had been nibbling away in the darkness like mice and cockroaches hurriedly scuttled for cover. That was when I learned that worship and worry cannot live in the same heart: they are mutually exclusive.

219

As a teacher, you are presented daily with challenges and situations that can be worrisome. Choose to turn these cares over to the Lord and worship Him instead. Praise Him for His faithfulness, and trust Him to provide the answers you need.

Endnotes

1   (p. 9) Glenn Van Ekeren, *Words for All Occasions* (Paramus, New Jersey: Prentice Hall, 1988) p. 54.

2   (p. 11) Charles J. Givens, *Super Self* (New York: Simon & Schuster, 1993) pp. 188-189.

3   (p. 21) Glenn Van Ekeren, *Words for All Occasions* (Paramus, New Jersey: Prentice Hall, 1988) pp. 35-36, 198-199.

4   (p. 23) John. H. Timmerman, "Black Gold: Nurturing the Heart," *Moody* (September 1994) p. 14.

5   (p. 33) Craig Brian Larson, *Illustrations for Preaching and Teaching* (Grand Rapids, Michigan: Baker Books, 1993) entry 260.

6   (p. 37) "Heroes for Today," *Reader's Digest* (Pleasantville, New Jersey: Reader's Digest Association, June 1997) p. 101.

7   (p. 39) "Heroes for Today," *Reader's Digest* (June 1997) pp. 99-100.

8   (p. 47) Lillian Eichler Watson, *Light From Many Lamps* (New York: First Fireside/Simon & Schuster, 1979) pp. 45-46.

9   (p. 49) Glenn Van Ekeren, *Words for All Occasions* (Paramus, New Jersey: Prentice Hall, 1988) p. 204.

10 (p. 51) Steven R. Mosley, *God: A Biography* (Phoenix, Arizona: Questar, 1988) pp. 187-189.

11 (p. 53) Della Reese, *Angels Along the Way: My Life with Help from Above* (New York: G.P. Putnam's Sons, 1997)

12 (p. 55) Carrie Boyko and Kimberly Colen, *Hold Fast Your Dreams* (New York: Scholastic, Inc., 1996) pp. 11-18.

13 (p. 59) Steven R. Mosley, *God: A Biography* (Phoenix, Arizona: Questar Publishers, 1988) pp. 201-202.

14 (p. 61) Glenn Van Ekeren, *Words for All Occasions* (Paramus, New Jersey: Prentice Hall, 1988) p. 290.

15 (p. 63) Sheila Walsh with Evelyn Bence, *Bring Back the Joy* (Grand Rapids, Michigan: Zondervan Publishing House, 1998) pp. 47-49,71-72.

16 (p. 65) Craig Brian Larson, *Illustrations for Preaching and Teaching* (Grand Rapids, Michigan: Baker Books, 1993) p. 259.

17 (p. 67) Michael Hodgin, *1001 Humorous Illustrations of Public Speaking* (Grand Rapids, Michigan: Zondervan Publishing House, 1994) number 385.

18 (p. 75) Roger Connors, Tom Smith, and Craig Hickman *The Oz Principle* (Englewood Cliffs, New Jersey: Prentice Hall, 1994) p. 139.

19 (p. 91) Anna B. Mow, *Your Child* (Grand Rapids, Michigan: Zondervan Publishing House, 1971) p. 34.

20 (p. 93) Michael Hodgin, *1001 Humorous Illustrations of Public Speaking* (Grand Rapids, Michigan: Zondervan Publishing House, 1994) number 301; and from "Mikey's

Funnies" @ YOUTH SPECIALITIES, "A Christian's Kids,"
online at aol, 9/23/98.

[21] (p. 95) Alice Gray, *Stories for the Heart* (Sisters, Oregon:
Questar, 1996) p. 109.

[22] (p. 97) Robert L. Veninga, *Your Renaissance Years* (Boston:
Little, Brown & Co., 1991) pp. 237-238.

[23] (p. 101) Dr. Ray Guarendi, *Back to the Family* (New York:
Villard Books, Random House, 1990) pp. 162-163.

[24] (p. 103) Glenn Van Ekeren, *Words for All Occasions*
(Paramus, New Jersey: Prentice Hall, 1988) pp. 10-11.

[25] (p. 105) Craig Brian Larson, *Contemporary Illustrations for
Preachers, Teachers, and Writers* (Grand Rapids, Michigan:
Baker Books, 1996) number 138. Prisoner anecdote from
Michael Hodgin, *1001 Humorous Illustrations of Public
Speaking* (Grand Rapids, Michigan: Zondervan Publishing
House, 1994) number 650.

[26] (p. 107) Allan Cox, *Straight Talk for Monday Morning*
(New York: John Wiley & Sons, 1990) pp. 235-236.

[27] (p. 109) Paul Lee Tan, *Encyclopedia of 7700 Illustrations*
(Rockville, Maryland: Assurance Publishers, 1979)
pp. 678-679.

[28] (p. 111) Craig Brian Larson, *Contemporary Illustrations for
Preachers, Teachers, and Writers* (Grand Rapids, Michigan:
Baker Books, 1996) number 101. Article first appeared in
Guideposts (September 1980.)

[29] (p. 113) Tom Morris, *True Success* (New York:
Grosset/Putnam, 1994) p. 131.

[30] (p. 115) Charles Davis, *Parables Etc.* (April 1987). Found in
Michael Hodgin, *1001 Humorous Illustrations of Public
Speaking* (Grand Rapids, Michigan: Zondervan Publishing
House, 1994) number 520.

[31] (p. 121) James S. Hewett, *Illustrations Unlimited* (Wheaton,
Illinois: Tyndale House Publishers, 1988) p. 235.

[32] (p. 123) Richard A. Swenson, M.D., (Colorado Springs,
Colorado: NavPress Publishing Group, 1992) pp. 241-242.

[33] (p. 127) Alice Gray, *Stories for the Heart* (Sisters, Oregon:
Questar, 1996) pp. 75-76.

[34] (p. 131) Anna B. Mow, *Your Child* (Grand Rapids, Michigan:
Zondervan Publishing House, 1971) pp. 88-89.

[35] (p. 135) *Reader's Digest* (March 1996) p. 37.

[36] (p. 137) Craig Brian Larson, *Contemporary Illustrations for
Preachers, Teachers, and Writers* (Grand Rapids, Michigan:
Baker Books, 1996) number 156. Originally appeared as
"Epic in the Making," *Chicago Tribune* (December 1991)
Sec 5, Page 1.

[37] (p. 139) "Make Your Own Breaks," *Reader's Digest* (March
1996) p. 46.

[38] (p. 141) Charles Stanley, *The Wonderful Spirit-Filled Life*
(Nashville, Tennessee: Thomas Nelson Publishers, 1992)
pp. 48-49.

[39] (p. 143) E. Paul Hovey, *The Treasury of Inspirational Anecdotes, Quotations, and Illustrations* (Grand Rapids, Michigan: Fleming H. Revell, 1959) pp. 257-258.

[40] (p. 155) Sheila Walsh with Evelyn Bence, *Bring Back the Joy* (Grand Rapids, Michigan: Zondervan Publishing House, 1998) p. 145.

[41] (p. 169) Sheila Walsh with Evelyn Bence, *Bring Back the Joy* (Grand Rapids, Michigan: Zondervan Publishing House, 1998) pp. 150-151.

[42] (p. 171) Susan Hazen-Hammond, "Horny Toads Enjoy a Special Place in Western Hearts," *Smithsonian* (December 1994) p. 90.

[43] (p. 173) Craig Brian Larson, "Honest to God," *Contemporary Illustrations for Preachers, Teachers, and Writers* (Grand Rapids, Michigan: Baker Books, 1996) number 221, pp. 26-27.

[44] (p. 181) Craig Brian Larson, *Illustrations for Preaching and Teaching* (Grand Rapids, Michigan: Baker Books, 1993) p. 41.

[45] (p. 185) Charles J. Givens, *Super Self* (New York: Simon & Schuster, 1993) pp. 165-166.

[46] (p. 187) Robert S. Eliot, M.D., *From Stress to Strength—How to Lighten Your Load and Save Your Life* (New York: Bantam Books, 1994) pp. 49-51.

[47] (p. 189) Michael Hodgin, *1001 Humorous Illustrations for Public Speaking* (Grand Rapids, Michigan: Zondervan Publishing House, 1994) p. 319.

[48] (p. 191) Robert A. Wilson, *Character Above All* (New York: Simon & Schuster, 1995) p. 58.

[49] (p. 199) Alice Gray, *Stories for the Heart* (Sisters, Oregon: Questar, 1996) pp. 91-92.

[50] (p. 201) "Personal Glimpses," *Reader's Digest* (March 1996) p. 38.

[51] (p. 205) Craig Brian Larson, *Contemporary Illustrations for Preachers, Teachers, and Writers* (Grand Rapids, Michigan: Baker Books, 1996) number 181.

[52] (p. 207) Mark Victor Hansen and Barbara Nichols with Patty Hansen, *Out of the Blue* (New York: Harper Collins, 1996) pp. 100-102.

[53] (p. 209) Lou Holtz, *Winning Every Day—The Game Plan for Success* (New York: Harper Collins Publishers, 1998) p. 48.

[54] (p. 211) Barbara Bailey Reinhold, *Toxic Work* (New York: Penguin Books, 1996) pp. 58-60.

[55] (p. 213) Meg Cimino, "My Dad, The Worrier," *Reader's Digest* (June 1997) pp. 137-139. Originally from *The Atlantic Monthly* (March 1997).

[56] (p. 215) Donald Grey Barnhouse, *Let Me Illustrate* (Grand Rapids, Michigan: Baker Book House (Fleming H. Revell), 1967) p. 108.

Additional copies of this book and other
titles from Honor Books
are available at your local bookstore.

God's Little Lessons on Life
God's Little Lessons on Life for Dad
God's Little Lessons on Life for Graduates
God's Little Lessons on Life for Mom
God's Little Lessons for Leaders
God's Little Lessons for Teens
God's Little Lessons for Parents

If you have enjoyed this book,
or if it has impacted your life,
we would like to hear from you.

Please contact us at:

Honor Books
Department E
P.O. Box 55388
Tulsa, Oklahoma 74155
Or by e-mail at info@honorbooks.com